EVERYDAY
MIND

TRICYCLE BOOKS FROM RIVERHEAD

Breath Sweeps Mind: A First Guide to Meditation Practice
edited by Jean Smith

Everyday Mind: 366 Reflections on the Buddhist Path
edited by Jean Smith

Wake Up and Cook: Kitchen Buddhism in Words and Recipes
edited by Carole Tonkinson

Meeting the Buddha: On Pilgrimage in Buddhist India
edited by Molly Emma Aitken

Big Sky Mind: Buddhism and the Beat Generation
edited by Carole Tonkinson

Buddhism Without Beliefs: A Contemporary Guide to Awakening
by Stephen Batchelor

EVERYDAY MIND

366 REFLECTIONS ON THE BUDDHIST PATH

EDITED BY JEAN SMITH

A TRICYCLE BOOK

RIVERHEAD BOOKS, NEW YORK

Riverhead Books
Published by The Berkley Publishing Group
A member of Penguin Putnam Inc.
200 Madison Avenue
New York, New York 10016

First edition: November 1997

The Putnam Berkley World Wide Web site address is http://www.berkley.com

Library of Congress Cataloging-in-Publication Data
Everyday mind : 366 reflections on the Buddhist path / edited by Jean
    Smith. — 1st ed.
        p.   cm.
    "A tricycle book."
    ISBN 1-57322-633-5
    1. Buddhist devotional calendars.   2. Buddhist meditations.
I. Smith, Jean.
BQ5579.E94   1997
294.3'4432—dc21   97-3724
                                                                      CIP

Printed in the United States of America

10   9   8   7   6   5   4   3

For those who pull little red wagons
filled with stones,
and my Sangha-mate,
Julie, who has lightened hers

An Invitation

*"All of the Buddha's teachings are a
finger pointing at the moon."*

Twenty-five hundred years ago, a young aristocrat, Siddhartha Gautama, renounced his world of wealth and privilege and began a spiritual quest for the truth. After seeking this knowledge from respected teachers of his day, he found it in himself. He became the historic Buddha, "the Enlightened One."

For the next forty years, he traveled throughout northern India, teaching the truth of suffering and the end of suffering. He taught his followers the method of meditation and the practices that could lead to their own enlightenment. Repeatedly, he urged them to look inward, to look to their own experience for validation of his teachings. "All of the Buddha's teachings are a finger pointing at the moon"—they are not the moon, and if we stare at the finger rather than the direction it is pointing, we do not see the moon. By looking at the moon itself—at the truth in ourselves the Buddha showed us—we can truly deepen our own spiritual experience.

Many on this path have found that a daily spiritual practice is as necessary as daily physical nourishment and rest. The selections in *Everyday Mind* can be an integral part of practice. They focus on central Buddhist teachings: the Four Noble Truths of suffering and the end of suffering; the Eightfold Path and Precepts, which guide us in a life of nonharming; and aspects of meditation, the foundation of this practice. Written by Buddhists from various eras, places, and traditions, they reflect many paths to one truth. May the words be a finger pointing to each day.

Editor's note: Spellings have been retained from the original sources. Thus, you will find some terms expressed in one place in Pali, the language spoken in the Buddha's time, but in other places in Sanskrit, the language in which many of the teachings were recorded—for example, the Pali *Sutta, Dhamma,* and *Nibbana* and the Sanskrit *Sutra, Dharma,* and *Nirvana.* When teachings from classic sources are given and not otherwise attributed, the speaker is the Buddha.

Have confidence in your own spiritual potentiality, your ability to find your own unique way. Learn from others certainly, and use what you find useful, but also learn to trust your own inner wisdom. Have courage. Be awake and aware. Remember too that Buddhism is not about being a Buddhist; that is, obtaining a new identity tag. Nor is it about collecting head-knowledge, practices and techniques. It is ultimately about letting go of all forms and concepts and becoming free.

—John Snelling, *Elements of Buddhism*

A student once said: "When I was a Buddhist, it drove my parents and friends crazy, but when I am a buddha, nobody is upset at all."

—Jon Kabat-Zinn, *Wherever You Go, There You Are*

There is a simple way to become a buddha: When you refrain from unwholesome action, are not attached to birth and death, and are compassionate toward all sentient beings, respectful to seniors and kind to juniors, not excluding or desiring anything, with no designing thoughts or worries, you will be called a buddha. Do not seek anything else.

—Zen Master Dogen, *Moon in a Dewdrop,*
edited by Kazuaki Tanahashi

"Bhikkhus [Monks], before my enlightenment, while I was still only an unenlightened Bodhisattva, I too, being myself subject to birth, sought what was also subject to birth; being myself subject to aging, sickness, death, sorrow, and defilement, I sought what was also subject to aging, sickness, death, sorrow, and defilement. Then I considered thus: 'Why, being myself subject to birth, do I seek what is also subject to birth? Why, being myself subject to aging, sickness, death, sorrow, and defilement, do I seek what is also subject to aging, sickness, death, sorrow, and defilement? Suppose that, being myself subject to birth, having understood the danger in what is subject to birth, I seek the unborn supreme security from bondage, Nibbana [Nirvana]. Suppose that, being myself subject to aging, sickness, death, sorrow, and defilement, having understood the danger in what is subject to aging, sickness, death, sorrow, and defilement, I seek the unaging, unailing, deathless, sorrowless, and undefiled supreme security from bondage, Nibbana.'"

—Ariyapariyesana Sutta, in *The Middle Length Discourses of the Buddha,* trans. by Bhikkhu Bodhi

It is noteworthy . . . that the story of the Buddha's spiritual journey climaxes with his enlightenment but does not end there. Even as he was savoring the blissful state that followed his awakening, he was approached (in the traditional account) by a delegation of gods, who begged him to give up his private ecstasy so he could share his awakening with those who still suffered. This encounter and its outcome, however legendary, make the point that spiritual maturity includes the ability to actualize transcendent insight in daily life. The Buddha is said to have wandered across northern India for forty years, tirelessly teaching the dharma. His decision to arise from his seat under the Bo tree and go out into the world can be considered the first step of a socially engaged Buddhism. The Buddha's discourses, which had revolutionary force in the society of his time, include countless passages dealing with "this-worldly" topics such as politics, good government, poverty, crime, war, peace, and ecology.

—Kenneth Kraft, *Inner Peace, World Peace*

Just as the water flows under the ground
So those who seek it find it,
Without thought, without end,
Its effective power all-pervasive,
Buddha Knowledge is also like this,
Being in all creatures' minds;
If any work on it with diligence,
They will soon find the light of knowledge.

—*The Flower Ornament Scripture,*
trans. by Thomas Cleary

Imagine a very poor man living in a decrepit little shanty, the only thing he owns in the world. What he does not know is that just beneath his shanty, but hidden in the dirt, is an inexhaustible vein of gold. As long as he remains ignorant of his hidden wealth, this pauper remains in poverty; but when he attends more closely to his own dwelling, he is bound to discover his own fathomless wealth. Similarly, all we need to do is unveil our own nature, and we will find an inexhaustible source of wisdom, compassion, and power. It is nothing we need to acquire, from anywhere or anything. It has always been there.

Seen in this light, the Buddha-nature requires no additions. One does not have to memorize sutras, recite prayers, or accumulate virtues to create it. All one needs to do is unveil it.

—B. Alan Wallace, *Tibetan Buddhism from the Ground Up*

[We can] view the Buddha as a fundamental archetype of humanity; that is, as the full manifestation of buddha-nature, the mind that is free of defilement and distortion, and understanding his life story as a great journey representing some basic archetypal aspects of human existence. By viewing the life of the Buddha . . . as a historical person and as an archetype, it becomes possible to see the unfolding of universal principles within the particular content of his life experience. We can then view the Buddha's life not as an abstract, removed story of somebody who lived twenty-five hundred years ago, but as one that reveals the nature of the universal in us all. This becomes a way of understanding our own experience in a larger and more profound context, one that connects the Buddha's journey with our own. We have undertaken to follow the same path, motivated by the same questions: What is the true nature of our lives? What is the root cause of our suffering?

—Joseph Goldstein, *Seeking the Heart of Wisdom*

The first noble truth says simply that it's part of being human to feel discomfort. We don't even have to call it suffering anymore; we don't even have to call it discomfort. It's simply coming to know the fieriness of fire, the wildness of wind, the turbulence of water, the upheaval of earth, as well as the warmth of fire, the coolness and smoothness of water, the gentleness of the breezes, and the goodness, solidity, and dependability of the earth. Nothing in its essence is one way or the other. The four elements take on different qualities; they're like magicians. Sometimes they manifest in one form and sometimes in another. . . . The first noble truth recognizes that we also change like the weather, we ebb and flow like the tides, we wax and wane like the moon.

—Pema Chödrön, *Awakening Loving-Kindness*

The venerable [disciple] Sariputta said this: "Friends, just as the footprint of any living being that walks can be placed within an elephant's footprint, and so the elephant's footprint is declared the chief of them because of its great size; so too, all wholesome states can be included in the Four Noble Truths."

—Mahahhatthipadopama Sutta, in *The Middle Length Discourses of the Buddha,* trans. by Bhikkhu Bodhi

With regard to the Four Noble Truths we have four functions to perform:

The First Noble Truth is *Dukkha*, the nature of life, its suffering, its sorrows and joys, its imperfection and unsatisfactoriness, its impermanence and insubstantiality. With regard to this, our function is to understand it as a fact, clearly and completely.

The Second Noble Truth is the Origin of *Dukkha*, which is desire, "thirst," accompanied by all other passions, defilements and impurities. A mere understanding of this fact is not sufficient. Here our function is to discard it, to eliminate, to destroy and eradicate it.

The Third Noble Truth is the Cessation of *Dukkha*, Nirvana, the Absolute Truth, the Ultimate Reality. Here our function is to realize it.

The Fourth Noble Truth is the Path leading to the realization of Nirvana. A mere knowledge of the Path, however complete, will not do. In this case, our function is to follow it and keep to it.

—Walpola Rahula, *What the Buddha Taught*

Munindra-ji used to say that in spiritual practice, time is not a factor. Practice cannot be measured in time, so let go of the whole notion of when and how long. The practice is a process unfolding, and it unfolds in its own time. It is like the flowers that grow in the spring. Do you pull them up to make them grow faster? I once tried to do that with carrots in my first garden when I was eight years old. It does not work.

We do not need any particular length of time for this process of letting things be.

—Joseph Goldstein, *Insight Meditation*

While we may concentrate on one particular aspect of the path at a time, it is important to have an overall balance between the different aspects. Meditation should progress hand in hand with study, without either one being neglected. Having cleared away doubts intellectually, we should integrate our understanding with the experience of meditation. In this way our practice will be balanced and complete.

—The Dalai Lama, *A Flash of Lightning in the Dark of Night*

When we take the one seat on our meditation cushion we become our own monastery. We create the compassionate space that allows for the arising of all things: sorrows, loneliness, shame, desire, regret, frustration, happiness.

Spiritual transformation is a profound process that doesn't happen by accident. We need a repeated discipline, a genuine training, in order to let go of our old habits of mind and to find and sustain a new way of seeing. To mature on the spiritual path we need to commit ourselves in a systematic way. My teacher Achaan Chah described this commitment as "taking the one seat." He said, "Just go into the room and put one chair in the center. Take the seat in the center of the room, open the doors and the windows, and see who comes to visit. You will witness all kinds of scenes and actors, all kinds of temptations and stories, everything imaginable. Your only job is to stay in your seat. You will see it all arise and pass, and out of this, wisdom and understanding will come."

—Jack Kornfield, *A Path with Heart*

When we practice zazen [Zen meditation] our mind always follows our breathing. When we inhale, the air comes into the inner world. When we exhale, the air goes out to the outer world. The inner world is limitless, and the outer world is also limitless. We say "inner world" or "outer world," but actually there is just one whole world. In this limitless world, our throat is like a swinging door. The air comes in and goes out like someone passing through a swinging door. If you think, "I breathe," the "I" is extra. There is no you to say "I." What we call "I" is just a swinging door which moves when we inhale and when we exhale. It just moves; that is all. When your mind is pure and calm enough to follow this movement, there is nothing: no "I," no world, no mind nor body; just a swinging door.

—Shunryu Suzuki, *Zen Mind, Beginner's Mind*

If you do decide to start meditating, there's no need to tell other people about it, or talk about why you are doing it or what it's doing for you. In fact, there is no better way to waste your nascent energy and enthusiasm for practice and thwart your efforts so they will be unable to gather momentum. Best to meditate without advertising it.

Every time you get a strong impulse to talk about meditation and how wonderful it is, or how hard it is, or what it's doing for you these days, or what it's not, or you want to convince someone else how wonderful it would be for them, just look at it as more thinking and go meditate some more. The impulse will pass and everybody will be better off—especially you.

—Jon Kabat-Zinn, *Wherever You Go, There You Are*

There's an old Zen story: a student said to Master Ichu, "Please write for me something of great wisdom." Master Ichu picked up his brush and wrote one word: "Attention." The student said, "Is that all?" The master wrote, "Attention Attention." . . .

For "attention" we could substitute the word "awareness." Attention or awareness is the secret of life and the heart of practice. . . . [E]very moment in life is absolute itself. That's all there is. There is nothing other than this present moment; there is no past, there is no future; there is nothing but this. So when we don't pay attention to each little *this,* we miss the whole thing. And the contents of *this* can be anything. *This* can be straightening our sitting mats, chopping an onion, visiting one we don't want to visit. It doesn't matter what the contents of the moment are; each moment is absolute. That's all there is, and all there ever will be. If we could totally pay attention, we would never be upset. If we're upset, it's axiomatic that we're not paying attention. If we miss not just one moment, but one moment after another, we're in trouble.

—Charlotte Joko Beck, *Nothing Special: Living Zen*

There is a sign outside a casino in Las Vegas that says, "You must be present to win." The same is true in meditation. If we want to see the nature of our lives, we must actually be present, aware, awake. Developing samadhi [concentration] is much like polishing a lens. If we are looking to see the cells and workings of the body with a lens that has not been ground sufficiently, we will not see clearly. In order to penetrate the nature of the mind and body, we must collect and concentrate our resources and observe with a steady, silent mind. This is exactly what the Buddha did: he sat, concentrated his mind, and looked within. To become a yogi, an explorer of the heart and mind, we must develop this capacity as well.

—Jack Kornfield, *Seeking the Heart of Wisdom*

The river flows rapidly down the mountain, and then all of a sudden it gets blocked with big boulders and a lot of trees. The water can't go any farther, even though it has tremendous force and forward energy. It just gets blocked there. That's what happens with us, too; we get blocked like that. Letting go at the end of the out-breath, letting the thoughts go, is like moving one of those boulders away so that the water can keep flowing, so that our energy and our life force can keep evolving and going forward. We don't, out of fear of the unknown, have to put up these blocks, these dams, that basically say no to life and to feeling life.

—Pema Chödrön, *Tricycle: The Buddhist Review,* Vol. I, #1

The artist's dilemma and the meditator's are, in a deep sense, equivalent. Both are repeatedly willing to confront an unknown and to risk a response that they cannot predict or control. Both are disciplined in skills that allow them to remain focused on their task and to express their response in a way that will illuminate the dilemma they share with others.

And both are liable to similar outcomes. The artist's work is prone to be derivative, a variation on the style of a great master or established school. The meditator's response might tend to be dogmatic, a variation on the words of a hallowed tradition or revered teacher. There is nothing wrong with such responses. But we recognize their secondary nature, their failure to reach the peaks of primary imaginative creation. Great Art and Great Dharma both give rise to something that has never quite been imagined before. Artist and meditator alike ultimately aspire to an original creative act.

—Stephen Batchelor, *Tricycle: The Buddhist Review,* Vol. IV, #2

Central to the Buddha's teaching is the doctrine of anatman: "not-self." This does not deny that the notion of an "I" works in the everyday world. In fact, we need a solid, stable ego to function in society. However, "I" is not real in an ultimate sense. It is a "name": a fictional construct that bears no correspondence to what is really the case. Because of this disjunction all kinds of problems ensue.

Once our minds have constructed the notion of "I," it becomes our central reference point. We attach to it and identify with it totally. We attempt to advance what appears to be its interests, to defend it against real or apparent threats and menaces. And we look for ego-affirmation at every turn: confirmation that we exist and are valued. The Gordian Knot of preoccupations arising from all this absorbs us exclusively, at times to the point of obsession. This is, however, a narrow and constricted way of being. Though we cannot see it when caught in the convolutions of ego, there is something in us that is larger and deeper: a wholly other way of being.

—John Snelling, *Elements of Buddhism*

The way we define and delimit the self is arbitrary. We can place it between our ears and have it looking out from our eyes, or we can widen it to include the air we breathe, or at other moments we can cast its boundaries farther to include the oxygen-giving trees and plankton, our external lungs, and beyond them the web of life in which they are sustained.

—Joanna Macy, *World As Lover, World As Self*

The Buddha described what we call "self" as a collection of aggregates—elements of mind and body—that function interdependently, creating the appearance of woman or man. We then identify with that image or appearance, taking it to be "I" or "mine," imagining it to have some inherent self-existence. For example, we get up in the morning, look in the mirror, recognize the reflection, and think, "Yes, that's me again." We then add all kinds of concepts to this sense of self: I'm a woman or man, I'm a certain age, I'm a happy or unhappy person—the list goes on and on.

When we examine our experience, though, we see that there is not some core being to whom experience refers; rather it is simply "empty phenomena rolling on." It is "empty" in the sense that there is no one behind the arising and changing phenomena to whom they happen. A rainbow is a good example of this. We go outside after a rainstorm and feel that moment of delight if a rainbow appears in the sky. Mostly, we simply enjoy the sight without investigating the real nature of what is happening. But when we look more deeply, it becomes clear that there is no "thing" called "rainbow" apart from the particular conditions of air and moisture and light.

Each one of us is like that rainbow—an appearance, a magical display, arising out our various elements of mind and body.

—Joseph Goldstein, *Tricycle: The Buddhist Review,* Vol. VI, #3

"Let not a person revive the past
Or on the future build his hopes;
For the past has been left behind
And the future has not been reached.
Instead with insight let him see
Each presently arisen state;
Let him know that and be sure of it,
Invincibly, unshakeably.
Today the effort must be made;
Tomorrow Death may come, who knows?
No bargain with Mortality
Can keep him and his hordes away.
But one who dwells thus ardently,
Relentlessly, by day, by night—
It is he, the Peaceful Sage has said,
Who has one fortunate attachment."

—Lomasakangiyabhaddekaratta Sutta, in *The Middle Length Discourses of the Buddha,* trans. by Bhikkhu Bodhi

Buddhist practice requires the undertaking of five basic precepts as the minimum commitment to not harming others through our speech and actions. These precepts are recited regularly to remind students of their commitment. The precepts are:

I undertake to refrain from killing and harming living
——beings.
I undertake to refrain from stealing and taking that which
——is not mine.
I undertake to refrain from causing harm through sexual
——misconduct.
I undertake to refrain from false speech, harmful speech,
——gossip, and slander.
I undertake to refrain from the misuse of intoxicants or
——substances such as alcohol or drugs that cause
——carelessness or loss of awareness.

The positive power of virtue is enormous. When we don't live by these precepts, it is said we live like wild beasts; without them, all other spiritual practice is a sham. Imagine trying to sit down to meditate after a day of lying and stealing. Then imagine what a different world this would be if everyone kept even one precept—not to kill, or not to lie, or not to steal. We would truly create a new world order.

—Jack Kornfield, *A Path with Heart*

We can see that implicit in all five precepts is the age-old Indian principle of ahimsa: not harming—either others or oneself. We can safely extend this to the environment, the world as a whole and even to outer space. Nothing in fact falls outside the sphere of our moral responsibility. For instance, according to the Hua-yen school of Buddhist philosophy, which developed in medieval China, our every action affects the whole of the Universe.

The grave environmental problems we now face on Planet Earth stem directly from our ignorance of this fact. Yet, perplexingly, even as we begin to see what we are doing and what suffering it will bring down on both ourselves and our descendants, we find it very difficult to change our ways. Everyone is aware that it would be a good thing if there were fewer cars, but no one wants to give up their own!

—John Snelling, *Elements of Buddhism*

In simple terms, what does karma mean? It means that whatever we do, with our body, speech, or mind, will have a corresponding result. Each action, even the smallest, is pregnant with its consequences. It is said by the masters that even a little poison can cause death, and even a tiny seed can become a huge tree. And as Buddha said: "Do not overlook negative actions merely because they are small; however small a spark may be, it can burn down a haystack as big as a mountain." Similarly he said: "Do not overlook tiny good actions, thinking they are of no benefit; even tiny drops of water in the end will fill a huge vessel." Karma does not decay like external things, or ever become inoperative. It cannot be destroyed "by time, fire, or water." Its power will never disappear, until it is ripened.

—Sogyal Rinpoche, *The Tibetan Book of Living and Dying*

The Buddha identified karma as volitional activity. That is, each volition in the mind is like a seed with tremendous potential. In the same way that the smallest acorn contains the potential of a great oak tree, so too each of our willed actions contains the seed of karmic results. The particular result depends on the qualities of mind associated with each volition. Greed, hatred, and delusion are unwholesome qualities that produce fruits of suffering; generosity, love, and wisdom are wholesome factors that bear fruits of happiness.

The Buddha called the understanding of this law of karma, the law of action and result, the "light of the world," because it illuminates how life unfolds and why things are the way they are. The wisdom of this understanding allows us the freedom to make wise choices in our life.

—Joseph Goldstein, *Insight Meditation*

There's a Zen story in which a man is enjoying himself on a river at dusk. He sees another boat coming down the river toward him. At first it seems so nice to him that someone else is also enjoying the river on a nice summer evening. Then he realizes that the boat is coming right toward him, faster and faster. He begins to get upset and starts to yell, "Hey, hey watch out! For Pete's sake, turn aside!" But the boat just comes faster and faster, right toward him. By this time he's standing up in his boat, screaming and shaking his fist, and then the boat smashes right into him. He sees that it's an empty boat.

This is the classic story of our whole life situation.

—Pema Chödrön, *Start Where You Are*

A bodhisattva is an ordinary person who takes up a course in his or her life that moves in the direction of buddha. You're a bodhisattva, I'm a bodhisattva; actually, anyone who directs their attention, their life, to practicing the way of life of a Buddha is a bodhisattva.

—Kosho Uchiyama, *Opening the Hand of Thought*

The Great Way is obvious to all my friends. They point it out quite readily on request, sometimes without request. Their words are painful because they threaten my character. I have to choose between the Great Way and me. An easy choice on paper—a hard one in fact.

—Robert Aitken, *Encouraging Words*

Like a man floating in water
Who dies of thirst, afraid of drowning:
So are those who are learned
Who do not apply the teaching.

Like a person skilled in medicine
Who can't cure his own disease:
So are those who are learned
Who do not apply the teaching.

Like a deaf musician
Who pleases others, not hearing himself:
So are those who are learned
Who do not apply the teaching.

Like someone on a corner
Saying all kinds of fine things,
While having no real inner virtue
So are those who don't practice.

—*The Flower Ornament Scripture,* trans. by Thomas Cleary

In Buddhism there are numerous paths of spiritual training. Each has its unique goal, purpose, and benefits for oneself and others. But in order to be able to benefit truly, it is very important to understand the principal purpose underlying these practices. If we take the wrong turn at a crossroads, every step we make will take us farther away from our destination. In the same way, if we fail to realize the nature of our spiritual goal and what our aim should be, our practice will not be beneficial, or at least not nearly as helpful as it could otherwise be.

The main focus of all of our training in Dharma is to benefit our minds. . . . If we do not improve our minds, then regardless of how many understandings we have about the ten stages, the five paths, ceremonies, philosophies, and so forth, they'll all become objects that we never apply to ourselves. It can be very simple, like when we are facing the right direction— every step will bring us closer to our destination.

—Tulku Thondup, *Enlightened Journey*

The Buddha taught about four paths or roads to success, to fulfillment . . . They are four different qualities of character, each reflecting a different strength of personality. If we can recognize which of them is our own particular strength, then we can build on that power we already have; we can do what has to be done. . . .

We may free ourselves through the power of zeal, the great desire and motivation to follow the path; we may do it through the quality of heroic effort, an effort that cannot be stopped; we may come to awakening through our absorption in and love for the Dharma; or we may experience freedom through the power of investigation, the need to know and understand. Any one of these can be our path of fulfillment.

Our work is to recognize where our own strength lies, and to practice from that place of strength, to develop it, to cultivate it, and to make it even stronger. Our great life challenge is to do the work of awakening, to see that the path of practice lies in bringing these liberating qualities of heart and mind to each moment. . . . The Buddha pointed out the four roads to success. The rest is up to us.

—Joseph Goldstein, *Insight Meditation*

Practice is twofold. The first part is training; the second is the act itself. And these are not two things: when you train, the act itself is happening; when you are the act itself, your training is deepened.

Practice is to work "as if." The lawyer practices as if she or he were an attorney. The doctor practices as if she or he were a physician. Being and learning are one and the same.

It is just as though you were trying to play the piano with Mozart's hands. At first such action "as if" is awkward, but with practice your music becomes your own best creation. In the same way, your zazen becomes your own best inspiration, and your interaction with others expresses the love which has been in your heart from the very beginning.

—Robert Aitken, *Encouraging Words*

The core of Dharma practice is freeing oneself from the attachments of this life. It focuses on the deeper issue of gaining complete release from discontent by means of freeing our minds from the afflictions of confusion, attachment, and anger. In a broader sense, Dharma practice is concerned with serving others, in terms of both their temporary and ultimate needs.

Does this mean that one who is committed to Dharma suddenly renounces all worldly enjoyments—no more vacations, no entertainment, no sensory pleasures? No. If one tries that approach it usually results in spiritual burnout; and the common rebound is equally extreme sensual indulgence.

For this reason, the practice of Buddhist Dharma is often called *the Middle Way* because it seeks to avoid the extremes of sensual indulgence and severe asceticism. The former leads to perpetual dissatisfaction and the latter damages one's physical and mental health. . . . The Middle Way is a sensitive exertion of effort that is neither lax nor aggressive, and from this practice there ultimately arises an increasing satisfaction and delight in virtuous activity that is a result of our spiritual transformation.

—B. Alan Wallace, *Tibetan Buddhism from the Ground Up*

The supreme water spirit Ocean
Covers the earth with clouds;
The rain in each place is different,
But the spirit has no thought of distinction.
Likewise Buddha, sovereign of truth,
Extends clouds of great compassion in all directions,
Raining differently for each practitioner,
Yet without discriminating among them.

—*The Flower Ornament Scripture,* trans. by Thomas Cleary

[T]he Buddha compares his teaching to the rainfall that descends without discrimination on the earth. That this rain causes some seeds to grow into flowers and some into great trees implies no differentiation in the rain but rather is due to the capacities of the seeds that it nurtures. Thus, the teaching of the Buddha is of a single flavor but benefits beings in a variety of ways according to their capacity.

—Donald S. Lopez, Jr., *Buddhism in Practice*

We try so hard to hang on to the teachings and "get it," but actually the truth sinks in like rain into very hard earth. The rain is very gentle, and we soften up slowly at our own speed. But when that happens, something has fundamentally changed in us. That hard earth has softened. It doesn't seem to happen by trying to get it or capture it. It happens by letting go; it happens by relaxing your mind, and it happens by the aspiration and the longing to want to communicate with yourself and others. Each of us finds our own way.

—Pema Chödrön, *Start Where You Are*

[T]his enlightenment of the Buddha's was profound and brilliant, accurate and powerful, and also warm and compassionate. It was like the sun behind the clouds. Anyone who has taken off in an airplane on a grim and gloomy day knows that beyond the cloud cover the sun is always shining. Even at night the sun is shining, but then we can't see it because the earth is in the way, and probably our pillow also. The Buddha explained that behind the cloud cover of thoughts—including very heavy clouds of emotionally charged thoughts backed up by entrenched habitual patterns—there is continual warm, bright, loving intelligence constantly shining. And even though in the midst of thoughts, emotions, and habitual patterns, intelligence may become dulled and confused, it is still this intelligence in the midst of the thoughts and emotions and habits that makes them so very captivating, so resourceful and various, so inexhaustible.

—Samuel Bercholz, *Entering the Stream*

Most people think of enlightenment as a kind of magical attainment, a state of being close to perfection. At this level, one can perform amazing feats, see past and future lives of others, and tune in to the inner workings of the universe. This may be possible for a number of special beings, but for most of us enlightenment is much more in line with what Suzuki Roshi describes. It means having a quality of "beginningness," a fresh, simple, unsophisticated view of things. To have "beginner's mind" in how we approach things is a major teaching. In many ways, the process of enlightenment is clearing away the thoughts, beliefs, and ideas that cloud our ability to see things as they really are in their pristine form.

—David A. Cooper, *Silence, Simplicity and Solitude*

After you wake up, you probably open the curtains and look outside. You may even like to open the window and feel the cool morning air with the dew still on the grass. But is what you see really "outside"? In fact, it is your own mind. As the sun sends its rays through the window, you are not just yourself. You are also the beautiful view from your window. You are the *Dharmakaya.*

Dharmakaya literally means the "body" *(kaya)* of the Buddha's teachings *(Dharma),* the way of understanding and love. Before passing away, the Buddha told his disciples, "Only my physical body will pass away. My Dharma body will remain with you forever." In Mahayana Buddhism, the word has come to mean "the essence of all that exists." All phenomena—the song of a bird, the warm rays of the sun, a cup of hot tea—are manifestations of the Dharmakaya. We, too, are of the same nature as these wonders of the universe.

—Thich Nhat Hanh, *Present Moment, Wonderful Moment*

Most of the time we go through the day, through our activities, our work, our relationships, our conversations, and very rarely do we ground ourselves in an awareness of our bodies. We are lost in our thoughts, our feelings, our emotions, our stories, our plans.

A very simple guide or check on this state of being lost is to pay attention to those times when you feel like you are rushing. Rushing does not have to do with speed. You can rush moving slowly, and you can rush moving quickly. We are rushing when we feel as if we are toppling forward. Our minds run ahead of ourselves; they are out there where we want to get to, instead of being settled back in our bodies. The feeling of rushing is good feedback. Whenever we are not present, right then, in that situation, we should stop and take a few deep breaths. Settle into the body again. Feel yourself sitting. Feel the step of a walk. Be in your body.

The Buddha made a very powerful statement about this: "Mindfulness of the body leads to nirvana." Such awareness is not a superficial practice. Mindfulness of the body keeps us present.

—Joseph Goldstein, *Transforming the Mind, Healing the World*

Some people think that they will practice the dharma once they have finished with their worldly business. This is a mistaken attitude because our work in the world never finishes. Work is like a ripple of water continually moving on the surface of the ocean. It is very difficult to break free from our occupations in order to practice dharma. The busy work with which we fill our lives is only completed at the time of our death.

—Geshe Kelsang Gyatso, *Meaningful to Behold*

The practice of metta, uncovering the force of love that can uproot fear, anger, and guilt, begins with befriending ourselves. The foundation of metta practice is to know how to be our own friend. According to the Buddha, "You can search throughout the entire universe for someone who is more deserving of your love and affection than you are yourself, and that person is not to be found anywhere. You yourself, as much as anybody in the entire universe, deserve your love and affection." How few of us embrace ourselves in this way! With metta practice we uncover the possibility of truly respecting ourselves. We discover, as Walt Whitman put it, "I am larger and better than I thought. I did not think I held so much goodness."

—Sharon Salzberg, *Lovingkindness*

The essence of the Buddha's message is contained in the Four Noble Truths. The first of these is the truth of suffering. . . . The Buddha declared that all our experiences of joy, indifference, and pain are unsatisfactory. Are not even our greatest mundane pleasures tainted with dissatisfaction? When these pleasures pass away are we not left with unfulfilled longing and discontent? But in spite of this, we tend to cling to the pleasures of life, ignoring their transient nature. . . .

The suffering we must recognize includes not only the kind we experience at the loss of a loved one, or when we lose our job, for example, but also includes the more fundamental conditions of our human existence, namely, aging, sickness, and death.

—B. Alan Wallace, *Tibetan Buddhism from the Ground Up*

The First Noble Truth declares unflinchingly, straight out, that pain is inherent in life itself just because everything is changing. The Second Noble Truth explains that suffering is what happens when we struggle with whatever our life experience is rather than accepting and opening to our experience with wise and compassionate response. From this point of view, there's a big difference between pain and suffering. Pain is inevitable; lives come with pain. Suffering is not inevitable. If suffering is what happens when we struggle with our experience because of our inability to accept it, then suffering is an optional extra.

I misunderstood this when I started my practice and believed if I meditated hard enough I would be finished with all pain. That turned out to be a big mistake. I was disappointed when I discovered the error and embarrassed that I had been so naive. It's obvious we are not going to finish with pain in this lifetime.

The Buddha said, "Everything dear to us causes pain." . . . Those of us who have chosen relational life have made the choice that the pain is worth it.

—Sylvia Boorstein, *It's Easier Than You Think*

Seeing the suffering in the world around us and in our own bodies and minds, we begin to understand suffering not only as an individual problem, but as a universal experience. It is one of the aspects of being alive. The question that then comes to mind is: If compassion arises from the awareness of suffering, why isn't the world a more compassionate place? The problem is that often our hearts are not open to feel the pain. We move away from it, close off, and become defended. By closing ourselves off from suffering, however, we also close ourselves to our own wellspring of compassion. We don't need to be particularly saintly in order to be compassionate. Compassion is the natural response of an open heart, but that wellspring of compassion remains capped as long as we turn away from or deny or resist the truth of what is there. When we deny our experience of suffering, we move away from what is genuine to what is fabricated, deceptive, and confusing.

—Joseph Goldstein, *Seeking the Heart of Wisdom*

21. "And what, monks, is the Noble Truth of the Way of Practice Leading to the Cessation of Suffering? It is just this Noble Eightfold Path, namely: —Right View, Right Thought; Right Speech, Right Action, Right Livelihood; Right Effort, Right Mindfulness, Right Concentration."

—Mahasatipatthana Sutta: The Greater Discourse on the
Foundations of Mindfulness, in *Thus Have I Heard:
The Long Discourses of the Buddha,*
trans. by Maurice Walshe

The Eightfold Path of Right Views, Right Thoughts, Right Speech, Right Conduct [Action], Right Livelihood, Right Effort or Lifestyle, Right Recollection [Mindfulness], and Right Meditation [Concentration] was preached by the Buddha to his first five disciples at Benares, and it remains for us the basic guide for our lives as Buddhists. It begins with Right Views and ends with Right Meditation, but each element of the path depends on all others, so really there is no first step and no last step. The key word is "right," from words in Sanskrit and Chinese that mean "upright, straight, right, correct." Finding what is upright in attitude, thought, speech, action, livelihood, effort, mindfulness, and meditation, and then doing it—this is our life work.

—Robert Aitken, *Encouraging Words*

"And what, monks, is Right View? It is, monks, the knowledge of suffering, the knowledge of the origin of suffering, the knowledge of the cessation of suffering, and the knowledge of the way of practice leading to the cessation of suffering. This is called Right View."

—Mahasatipatthana Sutta: The Greater Discourse on the Foundations of Mindfulness, in *Thus Have I Heard: The Long Discourses of the Buddha*, trans. by Maurice Walshe

"And what, monks, is Right Thought? The thought of renunciation, the thought of non-ill-will, the thought of harmlessness.
This, monks, is called Right Thought."

—Mahasatipatthana Sutta: The Greater Discourse on the
Foundations of Mindfulness, in *Thus Have I Heard:
The Long Discourses of the Buddha,*
trans. by Maurice Walshe

"And what, monks, is Right Speech? Refraining from lying, refraining from slander, refraining from harsh speech, refraining from frivolous speech. This is called Right Speech."

—Mahasatipatthana Sutta: The Greater Discourse on the
Foundations of Mindfulness, in *Thus Have I Heard:
The Long Discourses of the Buddha,*
trans. by Maurice Walshe

"And what, monks, is Right Action? Refraining from taking life, refraining from taking what is not given, refraining from sexual misconduct. This is called Right Action."

—Mahasatipatthana Sutta: The Greater Discourse on the
Foundations of Mindfulness, in *Thus Have I Heard:
The Long Discourses of the Buddha,*
trans. by Maurice Walshe

There are two criteria for right livelihood. First, it should not be necessary to break the five precepts in one's work, since doing so obviously causes harm to others. But further, one should not do anything that encourages other people to break the precepts, since this will also cause harm. Neither directly nor indirectly should our means of livelihood involve injury to other beings. Thus any livelihood that requires killing, whether of human beings or of animals, is clearly not right livelihood. . . . Selling liquor or other drugs may be very profitable, but even if one abstains from them oneself, the act of selling encourages others to use intoxicants and thereby to harm themselves. Operating a gambling casino may be very lucrative, but all who come there to gamble cause themselves harm. Selling poisons or weapons—arms, ammunition, bombs, missiles—is good business, but it injures the peace and harmony of multitudes. None of these is right livelihood.

Even though a type of work may not actually harm others, if it is performed with the intention that others should be harmed, it is not right livelihood. The doctor who hopes for an epidemic and the trader who hopes for a famine are not practicing right livelihood.

—S. N. Goenka, *The Art of Living*

"And what, monks, is Right Effort? Here, monks, a monk rouses his will, makes an effort, stirs up energy, exerts his mind and strives to prevent the arising of unarisen evil unwholesome mental states. He rouses his will . . . and strives to overcome evil unwholesome mental states that have arisen. He rouses his will . . . and strives to produce unarisen wholesome mental states. He rouses his will, makes an effort, stirs up energy, exerts his mind and strives to maintain wholesome mental states that have arisen, not to let them fade away, to bring them to greater growth, to the full perfection of development. This is called Right Effort."

—Mahasatipatthana Sutta: The Greater Discourse on the
Foundations of Mindfulness, in *Thus Have I Heard:
The Long Discourses of the Buddha,*
trans. by Maurice Walshe

"And what, monks, is Right Mindfulness? Here, monks, a monk abides contemplating body as body, ardent, clearly aware and mindful, having put aside hankering and fretting for the world; he abides contemplating feelings as feelings . . . he abides contemplating mind as mind . . . he abides contemplating mind-objects as mind-objects, ardent, clearly aware and mindful, having put aside hankering and fretting for the world. This is called Right Mindfulness."

—Mahasatipatthana Sutta: The Greater Discourse on the
Foundations of Mindfulness, in *Thus Have I Heard:
The Long Discourses of the Buddha,*
trans. by Maurice Walshe

"And what, monks, is Right Concentration? Here, a monk, detached from sense-desires, detached from unwholesome mental states, enters and remains in the first jhana [meditative absorption], which is with thinking and pondering, born of detachment, filled with delight and joy. And with the subsiding of thinking and pondering, by gaining inner tranquillity and oneness of mind, he enters and remains in the second jhana, which is without thinking and pondering, born of concentration, filled with delight and joy. And with the fading away of delight, remaining imperturbable, mindful and clearly aware, he experiences in himself the joy of which the Noble Ones say: 'Happy is he who dwells with equanimity and mindfulness,' he enters the third jhana. And, having given up pleasure and pain, and with the disappearance of former gladness and sadness, he enters and remains in the fourth jhana, which is beyond pleasure and pain, and purified by equanimity and mindfulness. This is called Right Concentration. And that, monks, is called the way of practice leading to the cessation of suffering."

—Mahasatipatthana Sutta: The Greater Discourse on the Foundations of Mindfulness, in *Thus Have I Heard: The Long Discourses of the Buddha,* trans. by Maurice Walshe

Suppose we use a traveling metaphor for the universal spiritual quest. The main map the Buddha offered for the trip to happiness and contentment is called the Eightfold Path, but I have often thought it should be called the Eightfold Circle. A path goes from here to there, and the nearer you are to *there,* the farther you are from *here*. A path is progressive . . . on a genuine path you would need to start at the beginning and proceed in a linear way until the end. With a circle, you can join in anywhere, and it's the same circle.

When the Buddha taught his path, he said it had a specific number of constituent parts; people could be sure they were going the right way if they saw any one of eight special markers. . . . The order in which the traveler sees the signs doesn't matter. If we look at any sign closely, it becomes apparent that each one has all of the others hidden inside it. Even a tiny bit of Right Understanding, the *suspicion* that it is possible to be contented even when we aren't pleased, arouses Right Aspiration to make a lot of Right Effort to develop more Right Understanding. . . . It's all connected.

—Sylvia Boorstein, *It's Easier Than You Think*

Remember that your thoughts are transformed into speech and action in order to bring the expected result. Thought translated into action is capable of producing a tangible result. You should always speak and do things with mindfulness of loving kindness. . . .

For all practical purposes, if all of your enemies are well, happy and peaceful, they would not be your enemies. If they are free from problems, pain, suffering, affliction, neurosis, psychosis, paranoia, fear, tension, anxiety, etc., they would not be your enemies. Your practical solution toward your enemies is to help them to overcome their problems, so you can live in peace and happiness. In fact, if you can, you should fill the minds of all your enemies with loving kindness and make all of them realize the true meaning of peace, so you can live in peace and happiness. The more they are in neurosis, psychosis, fear, tension, anxiety, etc., the more trouble, pain, and suffering they can bring to the world. If you could convert a vicious and wicked person into a holy and saintly individual, you would perform a miracle. Let us cultivate adequate wisdom and loving kindness within ourselves to convert evil minds to saintly minds.

—Henepola Gunaratana, *Mindfulness in Plain English*

I remember a short conversation between the Buddha and a philosopher of his time.

"I have heard that Buddhism is a doctrine of enlightenment. What is your method? What do you practice every day?"

"We walk, we eat, we wash ourselves, we sit down."

"What is so special about that? Everyone walks, eats, washes, sits down . . ."

"Sir, when we walk, we are aware that we are walking; when we eat, we are aware that we are eating. . . . When others walk, eat, wash, or sit down, they are generally not aware of what they are doing."

—Thich Nhat Hanh, *Zen Keys*

It is often the case that whatever we are doing, be it sitting, walking, standing, or lying, the mind is frequently disengaged from the immediate reality and is instead absorbed in compulsive conceptualization about the future or past. While we are walking, we think about arriving, and when we arrive, we think about leaving. When we are eating, we think about the dishes, and as we do the dishes, we think about watching television.

This is a weird way to run a mind. We are not connected with the present situation, but we are always thinking about something else. Too often we are consumed with anxiety and cravings, regrets about the past and anticipation for the future, completely missing the crisp simplicity of the moment.

—B. Alan Wallace, *Tibetan Buddhism from the Ground Up*

In the case of archery, the hitter and the hit are no longer two opposing objects, but are one reality. . . . Zen is the "everyday mind," as was proclaimed by Baso (Ma-tsu, died 788); this "everyday mind" is no more than "sleeping when tired, eating when hungry." As soon as we reflect, deliberate, and conceptualize, the original unconsciousness is lost and a thought interferes. We no longer eat while eating, we no longer sleep while sleeping. The arrow is off the string but does not fly straight to the target, nor does the target stand where it is. Calculation which is miscalculation sets in.

—D. T. Suzuki, in Eugen Herrigel's *Zen and the Art of Archery*

If we let a wild elephant loose in a populated area it will cause massive destruction, but the uncontrolled wild mind can cause much more harm than such a crazed beast. If the deluded, wild elephant of our mind is not subdued, it will create much suffering for us in this life and will cause us to experience the sufferings of the deepest hell in the future. In fact, if we investigate we can see that the creator of all the sufferings of this and future lives is nothing but our unsubdued mind. To subdue this wild beast is much more important than bringing a jungle elephant under our control.

Many benefits follow from taming our mind. If we take the rope of mindfulness and tie our elephant mind securely to the post of virtue, all of our fears will swiftly come to an end. . . .

If we do not develop mindfulness, our meditations will be hollow and empty. There will be nothing to keep our wild elephant mind from running back and forth in its customary, uncontrolled manner between objects of attachment, anger, jealousy and so forth.

—Geshe Kelsang Gyatso, *Meaningful to Behold*

Ancient Pali texts liken meditation to the process of taming a wild elephant. The procedure in those days was to tie a newly captured animal to a post with a good strong rope. When you do this, the elephant is not happy. He screams and tramples, and pulls against the rope for days. Finally it sinks through his skull that he can't get away, and he settles down. At this point you can begin to feed him and to handle him with some degree of safety. Eventually you can dispense with the rope and post altogether, and train your elephant for various tasks. Now you've got a tamed elephant that can be put to useful work. In this analogy the wild elephant is your wildly active mind, the rope is mindfulness, and the post is our object of meditation, our breathing. The tamed elephant who emerges from this process is a well-trained, concentrated mind that can then be used for the exceedingly tough job of piercing the layers of illusion that obscure reality. Meditation tames the mind.

—Henepola Gunaratana, *Mindfulness in Plain English*

1. Those who wish to guard their practice
   Should very attentively guard their minds,
   For those who do not guard their minds
   Will be unable to guard their practice.

2. In this (world) unsubdued and crazed elephants
   Are incapable of causing such harms
   As the miseries of the deepest hell
   Which can be caused by the unleashed elephant of my mind.

3. But if the elephant of my mind is firmly bound
   On all sides by the rope of mindfulness,
   All fears will cease to exist
   And all virtues will come into my hand.

—Shantideva, *A Guide to the Bodhisattva's Way of Life,*
trans. by Stephen Batchelor

As I left my daytime resting place on Vulture Peak,
I saw an elephant
come up on the riverbank after its bath.

A man took a hook and said to the elephant,
"Give me your foot."
The elephant stretched out its foot;
the man mounted.

Seeing what was wild before
gone tame under human hands,
I went into the forest
and concentrated my mind.

—Dantika, in Susan Murcott's *The First Buddhist Women*

We need to understand the concept of practice and what makes it spiritual. Practice is an activity that is regularly performed and is an open-ended process, never reaching a point of perfection. We can develop skills or even mastery with practice, but there always remains a quality of something new to learn.

If approached with a dull mind, even the most exotic practice becomes a rote expression. A person could spend a lifetime in practice this way and accomplish no more than a perfunctory exterior form without any spiritual substance. Unfortunately, many people find themselves following a traditional practice for the wrong reasons. They make all the right moves, but there is no heart in it.

We should approach the most mundane practice with a bright, open beginner's mind and regularly discover new insights, whether brushing our teeth, washing the dishes, or making the bed.

—David A. Cooper, *Silence, Simplicity and Solitude*

The life history of a butterfly is similar to our practice. We have some misconceptions about both, however. We may imagine, for example, that because butterflies are pretty, their life in the cocoon before they emerge is also pretty. We don't realize all that the worm must go through in order to become a butterfly. Similarly, when we begin to practice, we don't realize the long and difficult transformation required of us. We have to see through our pursuit of outward things, the false gods of pleasure and security. We have to stop gobbling this and pursuing that in our shortsighted way, and simply relax into the cocoon, into the darkness of the pain that is our life.

Such practice requires years of our lives. Unlike the butterfly, we don't emerge once and for all.

—Charlotte Joko Beck, *Nothing Special: Living Zen*

Every musician plays scales. When you begin to study the piano, that's the first thing you learn, and you never stop playing scales. The finest concert pianists in the world still play scales. It's a basic skill that can't be allowed to get rusty.

Every baseball player practices batting. It's the first thing you learn in Little League, and you never stop practicing. Every World Series game begins with batting practice. Basic skills must always remain sharp.

Seated meditation is the arena in which the meditator practices his own fundamental skills. The game the meditator is playing is the experience of his own life, and the instrument upon which he plays is his own sensory apparatus. Even the most seasoned meditator continues to practice seated meditation, because it tunes and sharpens the basic mental skills he needs for his particular game. We must never forget, however, that seated meditation itself is not the game. It's the practice. The game in which those basic skills are to be applied is the rest of one's experiential existence. Meditation that is not applied to daily living is sterile and limited.

—Henepola Gunaratana, *Mindfulness in Plain English*

Some people practice throughout their entire lives just by paying attention to breathing. Everything that is true about anything is true about breath: it's impermanent; it arises and it passes away. Yet if you didn't breathe, you would become uncomfortable; so then you would take in a big inhalation and feel comfortable again. But if you hold onto the breath, it's no longer comfortable, so you have to breathe out again. All the time shifting, shifting. Uncomfortableness is continually arising. We see that everything keeps changing.

—Sylvia Boorstein, *Tricycle: The Buddhist Review,* Vol. II, #1

Observing respiration is also the means for practicing right awareness. Our suffering stems from ignorance. We react because we do not know what we are doing, because we do not know the reality of ourselves. The mind spends most of the time lost in fantasies and illusions, reliving pleasant or unpleasant experiences and anticipating the future with eagerness or fear. While lost in such cravings or aversions, we are unaware of what is happening now, what we are doing now. Yet surely this moment, now, is the most important for us. We cannot live in the past; it is gone. Nor can we live in the future; it is forever beyond our grasp. We can live only in the present.

If we are unaware of our present actions, we are condemned to repeating the mistakes of the past and can never succeed in attaining our dreams for the future. But if we can develop the ability to be aware of the present moment, we can use the past as a guide for ordering our actions in the future, so that we may attain our goal.

—S. N. Goenka, *The Art of Living*

There's a story of three people who are watching a monk standing on top of a hill. After they watch him for a while, one of the three says, "He must be a shepherd looking for a sheep he's lost." The second person says, "No, he's not looking around. I think he must be waiting for a friend." And the third person says, "He's probably a monk. I'll bet he's meditating." They begin arguing over what this monk is doing, and eventually, to settle the squabble, they climb up the hill and approach him. "Are you looking for a sheep?" "No, I don't have any sheep to look for." "Oh, then you must be waiting for a friend." "No, I'm not waiting for anyone." "Well, then you must be meditating." "Well, no. I'm just standing here. I'm not doing anything at all."

. . . [S]eeing Buddha-nature requires that we . . . completely be each moment, so that whatever activity we are engaged in—whether we're looking for a lost sheep, or waiting for a friend, or meditating—we are standing right here, right now, doing nothing at all.

—Charlotte Joko Beck, *Everyday Zen*

The Dharma of the Buddha is not found in books. If you want to really see for yourself what the Buddha was talking about you don't need to bother with books. Watch your own mind. Examine to see how feelings come and go, how thoughts come and go. Don't be attached to anything, just be mindful of whatever there is to see. This is the way to the truths of the Buddha. Be natural. Everything you do in your life here is a chance to practice. It is all Dharma. When you do your chores try to be mindful. If you are emptying a spittoon or cleaning a toilet don't feel you are doing it as a favor for anyone else. There is Dharma in emptying spittoons. Don't feel you are practicing only when sitting still cross-legged. Some of you have complained that there is not enough time to meditate. Is there enough time to breathe? This is your meditation: mindfulness, naturalness in whatever you do.

—Achaan Chaa, in Jack Kornfield's *Living Dharma*

19. "And what, monks, is the Noble Truth of the Origin of Suffering? It is that craving which gives rise to rebirth, bound up with pleasure and lust, finding fresh delight now here, now there: that is to say sensual craving, craving for existence, and craving for non-existence.

"And where does this craving arise and establish itself? Wherever in the world there is anything agreeable and pleasurable, there this craving arises and establishes itself.

"And what is there in the world that is agreeable and pleasurable? The eye in the world is agreeable and pleasurable, the ear . . . the nose . . . the tongue . . . the body . . . the mind in the world is agreeable and pleasurable, and there this craving arises and establishes itself. Sights, sounds, smells, tastes, tangibles, mind-objects in the world are agreeable and pleasurable, and there this craving arises and establishes itself."

—Mahasatipatthana Sutta: The Greater Discourse on the
Foundations of Mindfulness, in *Thus Have I Heard:
The Long Discourses of the Buddha,*
trans. by Maurice Walshe

20. "And what, monks, is the Noble Truth of the Cessation of Suffering? It is the complete fading-away and extinction of this craving, its forsaking and abandonment, liberation from it, detachment from it. And how does this craving come to be abandoned, how does its cessation come about?

"Wherever in the world there is anything agreeable and pleasurable, there its cessation comes about. And what is there in the world that is agreeable and pleasurable?

"The eye in the world is agreeable and pleasurable, the ear . . . the nose . . . the tongue . . . the body . . . the mind in the world is agreeable and pleasurable, and there this craving comes to be abandoned, there its cessation comes about."

—Mahasatipatthana Sutta: The Greater Discourse on the
Foundations of Mindfulness, in *Thus Have I Heard:
The Long Discourses of the Buddha,*
trans. by Maurice Walshe

The Buddha's teaching is all about understanding suffering—its origin, its cessation, and the path to its cessation. When we contemplate suffering, we find we are contemplating desire, because desire and suffering are the same thing.

Desire can be compared to fire. If we grasp fire, what happens? Does it lead to happiness? If we say: "Oh, look at that beautiful fire! Look at the beautiful colors! I *love* red and orange; they're my favorite colors," and then grasp it, we would find a certain amount of suffering entering the body. And then if we were to contemplate the cause of that suffering we would discover it was the result of having grasped that fire. On that information, we would hopefully, then let the fire go. Once we let fire go then we know that it is something not to be attached to. This does not mean we have to hate it, or put it out. We can enjoy fire, can't we? It is nice having a fire, it keeps the room warm, but we do not have to burn ourselves in it.

—Ajahn Sumedho, *Teachings of a Buddhist Monk*

As wax melts near a lit wick and burns, it emits light near the tip of the candle. For the most part, this place from which light is emitted remains the same and appears as a fixed shape; it is this seemingly unchanging shape that we refer to as flame. That which is called I is similar to the flame. Although both body and mind are an unceasing flow, since they preserve what seems to be a constant form, we refer to them as I. Therefore, actually there is no I existing as some substantial thing; there is only the ceaseless flow. . . . That there is this seemingly fixed form based on various conditions is interdependence.

—Kosho Uchiyama, *Opening the Hand of Thought*

The habit of ignoring our present moments in favor of others yet to come leads directly to a pervasive lack of awareness of the web of life in which we are embedded. This includes a lack of awareness and understanding of our own mind and how it influences our perceptions and our actions. It severely limits our perspective on what it means to be a person and how we are connected to each other and to the world around us. Religion has traditionally been the domain of such fundamental inquiries within a spiritual framework, but mindfulness has little to do with religion, except in the most fundamental meaning of the word, as an attempt to appreciate the deep mystery of being alive and to acknowledge being vitally connected to all that exists.

—Jon Kabat-Zinn, *Wherever You Go, There You Are*

If you are a poet, you will see clearly that there is a cloud floating in this sheet of paper. Without a cloud, there will be no rain; without rain, the trees cannot grow; and without trees, we cannot make paper. The cloud is essential for the paper to exist. If the cloud is not here, the sheet of paper cannot be here either. So we can say that the cloud and the paper *inter-are*. "Interbeing" is a word that is not in the dictionary yet, but if we combine the prefix "Inter-" with the verb "to be," we have a new verb, inter-be. . . .

Looking even more deeply, we can see ourselves in this sheet of paper too. This is not difficult to see, because when we look at a sheet of paper, it is part of our perception. Your mind is in here and mine is also. So we can say that everything is in here with this sheet of paper. We cannot point out one thing that is not here—time, space, the earth, the rain, the minerals in the soil, the sunshine, the cloud, the river, the heat. Everything co-exists with this sheet of paper.

—Thich Nhat Hanh, *Peace Is Every Step*

We make every effort to keep things as they are, because human beings, alone, lament transience. Yet no matter how we grieve or protest, there is no way to impede the flow of anything. If we but see things as they are and flow with them, we may find enjoyment in transience. Because human life is transient, all manner of figures are woven into its fabric.

—Shundo Aoyama, *Zen Seeds*

The foundation and initial goal of [our] transformation is avoiding doing harm to others. Whether alone or with others, we must strive to avoid doing harm either directly with our words or deeds or indirectly with our thoughts and intentions. We may injure others with abuse, slander, sarcasm, and deceit, or by acts of omission due to insensitivity and thoughtlessness. The most subtle way of harming others is indirectly by means of our thoughts, judgments, and attitudes. When the mind is dominated by hostility, we may be viciously attacking others with our thoughts. Although no apparent injury may be inflicted, these thoughts affect us internally and influence our way of interacting with others, and the long-term effect is invariably harmful. So the initial theme of Dharma practice is a nonviolent approach to our own lives, to other living beings, and to our environment. This is a foundation for spiritual practice, and can provide well-being for both ourselves and others.

On this basis of nonviolence we can look for ways to serve others keeping in mind that any work will be altruistic if our motivation is one of kindness and friendliness.

—B. Alan Wallace, *Tibetan Buddhism from the Ground Up*

Sometimes we think that to develop an open heart, to be truly loving and compassionate, means that we need to be passive, to allow others to abuse us, to smile and let anyone do what they want with us. Yet this is not what is meant by compassion. Quite the contrary. Compassion is not at all weak. It is the strength that arises out of seeing the true nature of suffering in the world. Compassion allows us to bear witness to that suffering, whether it is in ourselves or others, without fear; it allows us to name injustice without hesitation, and to act strongly, with all the skill at our disposal. To develop this mind state of compassion . . . is to learn to live, as the Buddha put it, with sympathy for all living beings, without exception.

—Sharon Salzberg, *Lovingkindness*

All results come from causes that have the ability to create them. If we plant apple seeds, an apple tree will grow, not chili. If chili seeds are planted, chili will grow, not apples. In the same way, if we act constructively, happiness will ensue; if we act destructively, problems will result. Whatever happiness and fortune we experience in our lives comes from our own positive actions, while our problems result from our own destructive actions.

According to Buddhism, there is no one in charge of the universe who distributes rewards and punishments. We create the causes by our actions, and we experience their results. We are responsible for our own experience. The Buddha didn't create the system of actions and their effects, in the same way that Newton didn't invent gravity. Newton simply described what exists. Likewise, the Buddha described what he saw with his omniscient mind to be the natural process of cause and effect occurring within the mindstream of each being. By doing this, he showed us how best to work within the functioning of cause and effect in order to experience happiness and avoid pain.

—Thubten Chodron, *Tricycle: The Buddhist Review,* Vol. VI, #3

1. What we are today comes from our thoughts of yesterday, and our present thoughts build our life of tomorrow: our life is the creation of our mind.

   If a man speaks or acts with an impure mind, suffering follows him as the wheel of the cart follows the beast that draws the cart.

2. What we are today comes from our thoughts of yesterday, and our present thoughts build our life of tomorrow: our life is the creation of our mind.

   If a man speaks or acts with a pure mind, joy follows him as his own shadow.

—*The Dhammapada,* trans. by Juan Mascaro

Rather than dividing thoughts into classes like "good" and "bad," Buddhist thinkers prefer to regard them as "skillful" versus "unskillful." An unskillful thought is one connected with greed, hatred, or delusion. These are the thoughts that the mind most easily builds into obsessions. They are unskillful in the sense that they lead you away from the goal of Liberation. Skillful thoughts, on the other hand, are those connected with generosity, compassion, and wisdom. They are skillful in the sense that they may be used as specific remedies for unskillful thoughts, and thus can assist you toward Liberation.

—Henepola Gunaratana, *Mindfulness in Plain English*

It's impossible to take note of your mind all of the time. You would tie yourself up in knots and run off the road. Instead of going to an extreme, begin by concentrating on one particular emotion in yourself. Choose the emotion that bothers you the most, or the one that is most prominent in you. . . .

For many people, anger is a good starting point because it is easily noticed and dissolves faster than most other emotions. Once you begin to watch your anger, you will make an interesting discovery. You will find that as soon as you know you are angry, your anger will melt away by itself. It is very important that you watch without likes or dislikes. The more you are able to look at your own anger without making judgments, without being critical, the more easily the anger will dissipate.

—Thynn Thynn, *Living Meditation, Living Insight*

48. Whenever there is attachment in my mind
    And whenever there is the desire to be angry,
    I should not do anything nor say anything,
    But remain like a piece of wood.
49. Whenever I have distracted thoughts, the wish to verbally
    belittle others,
    Feelings of self-importance or self-satisfaction;
    When I have the intention to describe the faults of others,
    Pretension and the thought to deceive others;
50. Whenever I am eager for praise
    Or have the desire to blame others;
    Whenever I have the wish to speak harshly and cause dispute;
    At (all) such times I should remain like a piece of wood.
51. Whenever I desire material gain, honor or fame;
    Whenever I seek attendants or a circle of friends,
    And when in my mind I wish to be served;
    At (all) these times I should remain like a piece of wood.
52. Whenever I have the wish to decrease or to stop working
    for others
    And the desire to pursue my welfare alone . . .
53. Whenever I have impatience, laziness, cowardice,
    Shamelessness or the desire to talk nonsense;
    If thoughts of partiality arise,
    At these times too I should remain like a piece of wood.

—Shantideva, *A Guide to the Bodhisattva's Way of Life,*
    trans. by Stephen Batchelor

Shantideva . . . mentions specific instances when it is advisable to remain like a mindless piece of wood. We can do this when our mind is very distracted or when the thought arises to belittle, slander, or abuse others. If pride, haughtiness or the intention to find fault with others arises, we can also remain impassive until our deluded motivation fades. Feeling pretentious, thinking to deceive others and wishing to praise our own qualities, wealth, or possessions are all occasions when it is wise to pretend that we are made out of wood. Whenever we have the desire to blame others, speak harshly or cause disruption we should practise this technique of non-reaction.

—Geshe Kelsang Gyatso, *Meaningful to Behold*

If ye wonder whether evil *karma* can be neutralized or not,
Then know that it is neutralized by desire for goodness.
But they who knowingly do evil deeds,
Exchange a mouthful of food for infamy.
They who knowing not whither they themselves are bound,
Yet presume to pose as guides for others,
Do injury both to themselves and others.
If pain and sorrow ye desire sincerely to avoid,
Avoid, then, doing harm to others.

—W. Y. Evans-Wentz, *Tibet's Great Yogi Milarepa*

Most writings on the doctrine of karma emphasize the strict lawfulness governing karmic actions, ensuring a close correspondence between our deeds and their fruits. While this emphasis is perfectly in place, there is another side to the working of karma—a side rarely noted, but so important that it deserves to be stressed and discussed as an explicit theme in itself. This is the modifiability of karma, the fact that the lawfulness which governs karma does not operate with mechanical rigidity but allows for a considerably wide range of modifications in the ripening of the fruit.

If karmic action were always to bear fruits of invariably the same magnitude, and if modification or annulment of karma-result were excluded, liberation from the samsaric cycle of suffering would be impossible; for an inexhaustible past would ever throw up new obstructive results of unwholesome karma.

—Nyanaponika Thera, *The Heart of Buddhist Meditation*

Upon the oxen of a mind free from doubt
I put the yoke and plow of skillful means and wisdom.
Steadfastly I hold the reins without distraction.
Cracking the whip of effort, I break up the clods of the five
    poisons.
I cast away the stones of a defiled heart,
And weed out all hypocrisy.
I cut the stalks and reap the fruit of action
Leading to liberation. . . .
Realization does not arise out of words.
Understanding does not come from mere suggestions.
I urge all those who work for Enlightenment
To meditate with perseverance and effort.
Endurance and effort overcome the greatest of difficulties.
May there be no obstacles for those who seek Enlightenment.

—*The Life of Milarepa*, trans. by Lobsang P. Lhalunga

Cultivating the mind is very much like cultivating a crop. A farmer must know the proper way to prepare the soil, sow the seed, tend to the growth of the crop, and finally harvest it. If all these tasks are done properly, the farmer will reap the best harvest that nature allows. If they're done improperly, an inferior harvest will be produced, regardless of the farmer's hopes and anxieties.

Similarly, in terms of meditation it is crucial to be thoroughly versed in the proper method of our chosen technique. While engaged in the practice, we must frequently check up to see whether we are implementing the instructions we have heard and conceptually understood. Like a good crop, good meditation cannot be forced, and requires cultivation over time.

—B. Alan Wallace, *Tibetan Buddhism from the Ground Up*

Buddha was not interested in the elements comprising human beings, nor in metaphysical theories of existence. He was more concerned about how he himself existed in this moment. That was his point. Bread is made from flour. How flour becomes bread when put in the oven was for Buddha the most important thing. How we become enlightened was his main interest. The enlightened person is some perfect, desirable character, for himself and for others. Buddha wanted to find out how human beings develop this ideal character—how various sages in the past became sages. In order to find out how dough became perfect bread, he made it over and over again, until he became quite successful. That was his practice.

—Shunryu Suzuki, *Zen Mind, Beginner's Mind*

In spiritual life there is no room for compromise. Awakening is not negotiable; we cannot bargain to hold on to things that please us while relinquishing things that do not matter to us. A lukewarm yearning for awakening is not enough to sustain us through the difficulties involved in letting go. It is important to understand that anything that can be lost was never truly ours, anything that we deeply cling to only imprisons us.

—Christina Feldman and Jack Kornfield,
Stories of the Spirit, Stories of the Heart

It is possible to take our existence as a "sacred world," to take this place as open space rather than claustrophobic dark void. It is possible to take a friendly relationship to our ego natures, it is possible to appreciate the aesthetic play of forms in emptiness, and to exist in this place like majestic kings of our own consciousness. But to do that, we would have to give up grasping to make everything come out the way we daydream it should. So, suffering is caused by ignorance, or suffering exaggerated by ignorance or ignorant grasping and clinging to our notion of what we think should be, is what causes the "suffering of suffering." The suffering itself is not so bad, it's the resentment against suffering that is the real pain.

—Allen Ginsberg, *Tricycle: The Buddhist Review,* Vol. II, #1

Imagine walking along a sidewalk with your arms full of groceries, and someone roughly bumps into you so that you fall and your groceries are strewn over the ground. As you rise up from the puddle of broken eggs and tomato juice, you are ready to shout out, "You idiot! What's wrong with you? Are you blind?" But just before you can catch your breath to speak, you see that the person who bumped you is actually blind. He, too, is sprawled in the spilled groceries, and your anger vanishes in an instant, to be replaced by sympathetic concern: "Are you hurt? Can I help you up?"

Our situation is like that. When we clearly realize that the source of disharmony and misery in the world is ignorance, we can open the door of wisdom and compassion. Then we are in a position to heal ourselves and others.

—B. Alan Wallace, *Tibetan Buddhism from the Ground Up*

In Pali, heart and mind are one word *(citta)*, but in English we have to differentiate between the two to make the meaning clear. When we attend to the mind, we are concerned with the thinking process and the intellectual understanding that derives from knowledge, and with our ability to retain knowledge and make use of it. When we speak of "heart" we think of feelings and emotions, our ability to respond with our fundamental being. Although we may believe that we are leading our lives according to our thinking process, that is not the case. If we examine this more closely, we will find that we are leading our lives according to our feelings and that our thinking is dependent upon our feelings. The emotional aspect of ourselves is of such great importance that its purification is the basis for a harmonious and peaceful life, and also for good meditation.

—Ayya Khema, *When the Iron Eagle Flies*

A Zen poem says, "After the wind stops I see a flower falling. Because of the singing bird I find the mountain calmness." Before something happens in the realm of calmness, we do not feel the calmness; only when something happens within it do we find the calmness. There is a Japanese saying, "For the moon; there is the cloud. For the flower there is the wind." When we see a part of the moon covered by a cloud, or a tree, or a weed, we feel how round the moon is. But when we see the clear moon without anything covering it, we do not feel that roundness the same way we do when we see it through something else.

When you are doing zazen, you are within the complete calmness of your mind; you do not feel anything. You just sit. But the calmness of your sitting will encourage you in your everyday life. . . . Even though you do not feel anything when you sit, if you do not have this zazen experience, you cannot find anything; you just find weeds, or trees, or clouds in your daily life; you do not see the moon.

—Shunryu Suzuki, *Zen Mind, Beginner's Mind*

When we sit down to meditate, we are trying to transcend our everyday consciousness: the one with which we transact our ordinary business, the one used in the world's market-place as we go shopping, bring up our children, work in an office or in our business, clean the house, check our bank statements, and all the rest of daily living. That kind of consciousness is known to everyone and without it we can't function. It is our survival consciousness and we need it for that. It cannot reach far enough or deep enough into the Buddha's teachings, because these are unique and profound; our everyday consciousness is neither unique nor profound, it's just utilitarian.

In order to attain the kind of consciousness that is capable of going deeply enough into the teachings to make them our own and thereby change our whole inner view, we need a mind with the ability to remove itself from the ordinary thinking process. That is only possible through meditation. There is no other way. Meditation is therefore a means and not an end in itself. It is a means to change the mind's capacity in such a way that we can see entirely different realities from the ones we are used to.

—Ayya Khema, *When the Iron Eagle Flies*

Let the mind unite in a single point and let that composed mind dwell with the breath. Let the breath be its sole object of knowledge. Concentrate until the mind becomes increasingly subtle, until feelings are insignificant and there is great inner clarity and wakefulness. Then when painful sensations arise they will gradually cease of their own accord. Finally you'll look on the breath as if it was a relative come to visit you. When a relative leaves, we follow him out and see him off. We watch until he's walked or driven out of sight, and then we go back indoors. We watch the breath in the same way. If the breath is coarse, we know that it's coarse; if it's subtle, we know that it's subtle. As it becomes increasingly fine, we keep following it, while simultaneously awakening the mind. Eventually the breath disappears altogether and all that remains is the feeling of wakefulness. This is called meeting the Buddha.

—Ajahn Chah, in Samuel Bercholz's *Entering the Stream*

Once you have located your own breath point with clarity, don't deviate from that spot. Use this single point in order to keep your attention fixed. Without having selected such a point, you will find yourself moving in and out of the nose, going up and down the windpipe, eternally chasing after the breath, which you can never catch because it keeps changing, moving, and flowing. If you ever sawed wood you already know the trick. As a carpenter, you don't stand there watching the saw blade going up and down. You would get dizzy. You fix your attention on the spot where the teeth of the blade dig into the wood. It is the only way you can saw a straight line. As a meditator, you focus your attention on that single spot of sensation inside the nose. From this vantage point, you watch the entire movement of breath with clear and collected attention.

—Henepola Gunaratana, *Mindfulness in Plain English*

When people start to meditate or to work with any kind of spiritual discipline, they often think that somehow they're going to improve, which is a sort of subtle aggression against who they really are. It's a bit like saying, "If I jog, I'll be a much better person." "If I could only get a nicer house, I'd be a better person." "If I could meditate and calm down, I'd be a better person." . . .

But loving-kindness—*maitri*—toward ourselves doesn't mean getting rid of anything. Maitri means that we can still be crazy after all these years. We can still be angry after all these years. We can still be timid or jealous or full of feelings of unworthiness. The point is not to try to change ourselves. Meditation practice isn't about trying to throw ourselves away and become something better. It's about befriending who we are already. The ground of practice is you or me or whoever we are right now, just as we are. That's the ground, that's what we study, that's what we come to know with tremendous curiosity and interest.

—Pema Chödrön, *The Wisdom of No Escape and the Path of Loving-Kindness*

An indispensable foundation for meditation practice is following certain moral precepts. It is a way of maintaining a basic purity of body, speech, and mind. The five precepts which should be followed are: not killing, which means refraining from knowingly taking any life, not even swatting a mosquito or stepping on an ant; not stealing, which means not taking anything which is not given; refraining from sexual misconduct . . . not lying or speaking falsely or harshly; and not taking intoxicants. . . . Following these precepts will provide a strong base for the development of concentration, and will make the growth of insight possible.

—Joseph Goldstein, *The Experience of Insight*

The precepts are enormously powerful. For instance, not to tell an untruth in any circumstance, alone could be one's whole and total practice. With regard to other beings, it means not misrepresenting anything, being totally mindful and aware of just what is being said and making it as direct and clear a reflection of the truth as one can perceive. . . . To carry this precept even further, if one practices the precept of truthfulness within oneself as well, not fooling oneself, not trying to look at things other than as they really are, seeing things mindfully, with full consciousness and awareness, this one precept becomes the whole and entire practice of Buddhism. Not only of Buddhism, but in fact of all religions. As soon as one becomes totally honest, automatically the wisdom of unselfishness arises. One becomes loving in a natural way because one is no longer trying to get or be something other than what is already true.

—Jack Kornfield, *Living Dharma*

"There was a king who had a very powerful elephant, able to cope with five hundred ordinary elephants. When going to war, the elephant was armed with sharp swords on his tusks, with scythes on his shoulders, spears on his feet, and an iron ball at his tail. The elephant-master rejoiced to see the noble creature so well equipped, and, knowing that a slight wound by an arrow in the trunk would be fatal, he had taught the elephant to keep his trunk well coiled up. But during the battle the elephant stretched forth his trunk to seize a sword. His master was frightened and consulted with the king, and they decided that the elephant was no longer fit to be used in battle. . . . [I]f men would only guard their tongues all would be well! Be like the fighting elephant who guards his trunk against the arrow that strikes in the center."

—Paul Carus, *The Gospel of Buddha*

Because speech is so predominant in our lives, and because our words are so consequential, learning the art of skillful communication needs to be a significant aspect of our Dharma practice.

The Buddha emphasized the importance of this when he included right speech as a distinct part of the path to awakening. Although there is great elaboration of right speech in the texts, it all condenses into two general principles: Is it true? Is it useful?

Practicing these principles in our practice fosters increasing sensitivity. We become attuned to subtleties of truth and falsehood. Are there times when we shade the truth, or exaggerate in some way? And are there times when our words may be true, but it is not the right time, place, or situation for them to be useful?

—Joseph Goldstein, *Insight Meditation*

I think a lot about the fact that the Buddha made a separate category for Right Speech. He could have been more efficient and included it in Right Action, since speaking is a form of action. For a while I thought it was separate because we speak so much. But then I changed my mind—some people *don't* speak a lot. Now, I think it's a separate category because speech is so potent. . . .

During the 1960s, when the social ethos was "letting it all hang out," I had recurrent fantasies about writing a book called *Holding It All In*. I think I was alarmed that people had overlooked how vulnerable each of us is. In recent years, I've revised my book title to *Holding It All In Until We've Figured Out How to Say It in a Useful Way*.

I believe we are obliged to tell the truth. Telling the truth is a way we take care of people. The Buddha taught complete honesty, with the extra instruction that everything a person says should be truthful *and* helpful.

—Sylvia Boorstein, *It's Easier Than You Think*

51. As a beautiful flower that is full of hue but lacks fragrance, even so fruitless is the well-spoken word of one who does not practice it.

—*The Dharmapada,* in Walpola Rahula's
What the Buddha Taught

[A] Buddhist goes before an image and offers flowers or incense not to the model but to the Buddha as the perfection; he goes as a mark of gratitude and reflects on the perfection of the Buddha, meditating on the transiency of the fading flowers. . . . But a genuine reverence for the Buddha is to be measured only by the extent to which one follows his teaching.

—Hammalawa Saddhatissa, *Buddhist Ethics*

Before we do anything, we should always ask ourselves whether we will be able to do it properly and complete it. If the answer is no, we should not start. Leaving tasks uncompleted creates a habit for the future. So once we have begun something, we should be sure not to go back on our decision.

Self-confidence is not to be confused with pride. Pride is thinking highly of oneself without good reason. Self-confidence is knowing that one has the ability to do something properly and being determined not to give up.

Ordinary beings are prepared to make a good deal of effort for relatively insignificant ends. We have promised to work for the immensely more important goal of liberating all beings, so we should cultivate great self-confidence, thinking, Even if I am the only one to do so, I will benefit all beings.

—The Dalai Lama, *A Flash of Lightning in the Dark of Night*

Pride is a mental factor causing us to feel higher or superior to others. Even our study of dharma can be the occasion for the delusion of pride to arise if we think that our understanding is superior to that of everyone else. Pride is harmful because it prevents us from accepting fresh knowledge from a qualified teacher. Just as a pool of water cannot collect on the tip of a mountain, so too a reservoir of understanding cannot be established in a mind falsely elevated by pride.

—Geshe Kelsang Gyatso, *Meaningful to Behold*

Right Aspiration is what develops in the mind once we understand that freedom of choice is possible. Life is going to unfold however it does: pleasant or unpleasant, disappointing or thrilling, expected or unexpected, all of the above! What a relief it would be to know that whatever wave comes along, we can ride it out with grace. If we got really good at it, we could be like surfers, delighting especially in the most complicated waves.

What Right Aspiration translates to in terms of daily action is the resolve to behave in a way that stretches the limits of conditioned response. If I want to build big biceps, I need to use every opportunity to practice lifting weights. If I want to live in a way that is loving and generous and fearless, then I need to practice overcoming any tendency to be angry or greedy or confused. Life is a terrific gym. Every situation is an opportunity to practice. In formal Buddhist language, this is called the cultivation of nonhatred, nongreed, and nondelusion.

—Sylvia Boorstein, *It's Easier Than You Think*

One sure clue as to whether we're being motivated by aspiration or expectation is that aspiration is always satisfying; it may not be pleasant, but it is always satisfying. Expectation, on the other hand, is always unsatisfying, because it comes from our little minds, our egos. Starting way back in childhood, we live our lives looking for satisfaction outside ourselves. We look for some way to conceal the basic fear that something is missing from our lives. We go from one thing to another trying to fill up the hole we think is there.

—Charlotte Joko Beck, *Everyday Zen*

How would you deal with the death of your spouse? How would you feel if you lost your mother tomorrow? Or your sister or your closest friend? Suppose you lost your job, your savings, and the use of your legs, on the same day; could you face the prospect of spending the rest of your life in a wheelchair? How . . . will you deal with your own death, when that approaches? You may escape most of these misfortunes, but you won't escape all of them. . . . You can suffer through things like that or you can face them openly—the choice is yours.

Pain is inevitable, suffering is not. Pain and suffering are two different animals. If any of these tragedies strike you in your present state of mind, you will suffer. . . . Buddhism does advise you to invest some of your time and energy in learning to deal with unpleasantness, because some pain is unavoidable. When you see a truck bearing down on you, by all means jump out of the way. But spend some time in meditation, too. Learning to deal with discomfort is the only way you'll be ready to handle the truck you didn't see.

—Henepola Gunaratana, *Mindfulness in Plain English*

The greatest art in spiritual life is one of finding balance. The entire teachings of the Buddha are summed up in his encouragement to find and travel the middle path. To seek neither the extremes of mortification and aversion for life, nor the extreme of indulgence, losing ourselves in pleasure-seeking. The balance between these two is the path of awakening and freedom. The path of balance is to be with what is true in life and to love that, to be committed to the truth on every level of our being.

—Christina Feldman and Jack Kornfield,
Stories of the Spirit, Stories of the Heart

The practice of mindfulness-awareness meditation does not take place in a vacuum. It happens within a certain context and point of view. In the Buddhist tradition, meditation is often presented in the context of view, meditation, and action. View is like the eyes, which provide vision and perspective; meditation is like the mind, with its openness and clarity; and action is like the limbs that enable us to move about in the world. Each of these three is essential, as a system of checks and balances. So we cultivate all three of them together in order to overcome the prejudice and narrow-mindedness of our visions, the restlessness of our minds, and the ineffectiveness of our actions.

—Judy Lief, *Tricycle: The Buddhist Review,* Vol. VI, #3

When you ride in a boat and watch the shore, you might assume that the shore is moving. But when you keep your eyes closely on the boat, you can see that the boat moves. Similarly, if you examine myriad things with a confused body and mind you might suppose that your mind and nature are permanent. When you practice intimately and return to where you are, it will be clear that nothing at all has unchanging self.

—Zen Master Dogen, *Moon in a Dewdrop,*
edited by Kazuaki Tanahashi

Life is like a movie. It is like an unfolding story that we read and interpret, while identifying with the stars (i.e., gods) and immersing ourselves in the drama. When we start to notice this, life becomes lighter. The monotony fades and the magic begins. For when we turn our attention to our bodies, feelings, perceptions, impulses, and consciousness, we find that we are woven of the quixotic threads of ongoing stories. For only such a self can create and be created. A fixed, intractable one is as good as dead.

—Stephen Batchelor, *Tricycle: The Buddhist Review,* Vol. IV, #2

When the Buddha said "Do not pursue the past," he was telling us not to be overwhelmed by the past. He did not mean that we should stop looking at the past in order to observe it deeply. When we review the past and observe it deeply, if we are standing firmly in the present, we are not overwhelmed by it. The materials of the past which make up the present become clear when they express themselves in the present. We can learn from them. If we observe these materials deeply, we can arrive at a new understanding of them. That is called "looking again at something old in order to learn something new."

If we know that the past also lies in the present, we understand that we are able to change the past by transforming the present. The ghosts of the past, which follow us into the present, also belong to the present moment. To observe them deeply, recognize their nature, and transform them, is to transform the past.

—Thich Nhat Hanh, *Our Appointment with Life*

The universe that we inhabit and our shared perception of it are the results of a common karma. Likewise, the places that we will experience in future rebirths will be the outcome of the karma that we share with the other beings living there. The actions of each of us, human or nonhuman, have contributed to the world in which we live. We all have a common responsibility for our world and are connected with everything in it.

—The Dalai Lama, *A Flash of Lightning in the Dark of Night*

Karma is often wrongly confused with the notion of a fixed destiny. It is more like an accumulation of tendencies that can lock us into particular behavior patterns, which themselves result in further accumulations of tendencies of a similar nature. . . . But it is not necessary to be a prisoner of old karma. . . .

Here's how mindfulness changes karma. When you sit, you are not allowing your impulses to translate into action. For the time being, at least, you are just watching them. Looking at them, you quickly see that all impulses in the mind arise and pass away, that they have a life of their own, that they are not you but just thinking, and that you do not have to be ruled by them. Not feeding or reacting to impulses, you come to understand their nature as thoughts directly. This process actually burns up destructive impulses in the fires of concentration and equanimity and non-doing. At the same time, creative insights and creative impulses are no longer squeezed out so much by the more turbulent, destructive ones. They are nourished as they are perceived and held in awareness.

—Jon Kabat-Zinn, *Wherever You Go, There You Are*

"To sum up: First, a vivid state of mental tranquillity and a sustaining energy together with a discerning intellect are indispensable requirements for attaining perfect insight. They are like the first steps of a staircase.

"Second, all meditation, with or without form, must begin from deeply aroused compassion and love. Whatever one does must emerge from a loving attitude for the benefit of others.

"Third, through perfect seeing, all discrimination is dissolved into a nonconceptual state.

"Finally, with an awareness of the void, one sincerely dedicates the results for the benefit of others. I have understood this to be the best of all ways."

—*The Life of Milarepa,* trans. by Lobsang P. Lhalunga

According to Buddhism for a man to be perfect there are two qualities that he should develop equally: compassion on one side, and wisdom on the other. Here compassion represents love, charity, kindness, tolerance and such noble qualities on the emotional side, or qualities of the heart, while wisdom would stand for the intellectual side or the qualities of the mind. If one develops only the emotional neglecting the intellectual, one may become a good-hearted fool; while to develop only the intellectual side neglecting the emotional may turn one into a hardhearted intellect without feeling for others. Therefore, to be perfect one has to develop both equally. That is the aim of the Buddhist way of life: in it wisdom and compassion are inseparably linked together. . . .

—Walpola Rahula, *What the Buddha Taught*

A good spiritual friend who will help us to stay on the path, with whom we can discuss our difficulties frankly, sure of a compassionate response, provides an important support system which is often lacking. Although people live and practice together, one-upmanship often comes between them. A really good friend is like a mountain guide. The spiritual path is like climbing a mountain: we don't really know what we will find at the summit. We have only heard that it is beautiful, everybody is happy there, the view is magnificent and the air unpolluted. If we have a guide who has already climbed the mountain, he can help us avoid falling into a crevasse, or slipping on loose stones, or getting off the path. The one common antidote for all our hindrances is noble friends and noble conversations, which are health food for the mind.

—Ayya Khema, *When the Iron Eagle Flies*

Only the walker who sets out toward ultimate things is a pilgrim. In this lies the terrible difference between tourist and pilgrim. The tourist travels just as far, sometimes with great zeal and courage, gathering up acquisitions (a string of adventures, a wondrous tale or two) and returns the same person as the one who departed. There is something inexpressibly sad in the clutter of belongings the tourist unpacks back at home.

The pilgrim is different. The pilgrim resolves that the one who returns will not be the same person as the one who set out. Pilgrimage is a passage for the reckless and subtle. The pilgrim—and the metaphor comes to us from distant times—must be prepared to shed the husk of personality or even the body like a worn out coat. A Buddhist dictum has it that "the Way exists but not the traveler on it." For the pilgrim the road is home; reaching your destination seems nearly inconsequential.

—Andrew Schelling, *Meeting the Buddha,*
edited by Molly Emma Aitken

When we are driving, we tend to think of arriving, and we sacrifice the journey for the sake of the arrival. But life is to be found in the present moment, not in the future. In fact, we may suffer more after we arrive at our destination. If we have to talk of a destination, what about our final destination, the graveyard? We do not want to go in the direction of death; we want to go in the direction of life. But where is life? Life can be found only in the present moment. Therefore, each mile we drive, each step we take, has to bring us into the present moment. This is the practice of mindfulness.

When we see a red light or a stop sign, we can smile at it and thank it, because it is a bodhisattva helping us return to the present moment. The red light is a bell of mindfulness. We may have thought of it as an enemy, preventing us from achieving our goal. But now we know the red light is our friend, helping us resist rushing and calling us to return to the present moment where we can meet with life, joy, and peace.

—Thich Nhat Hanh, *Present Moment, Wonderful Moment*

"Bhikkhus, suppose a man in the course of a journey saw a great expanse of water, whose near shore was dangerous and fearful and whose further shore was safe and free from fear, but there was no ferryboat or bridge going to the far shore. . . . And then the man collected grass, twigs, branches, and leaves and bound them together into a raft, and . . . got safely to the far shore. Then, when he had got across and had arrived at the far shore, he might think thus: 'This raft has been very helpful to me . . . Suppose I were to hoist it on my head or load it on my shoulder, and then go wherever I want.' . . . By doing so, would that man be doing what should be done with that raft?"

"No, venerable sir."

". . . So I have shown you how the Dhamma is similar to a raft, being for the purpose of crossing over, not for the purpose of grasping."

—Alagaddupama Sutta, in *The Middle Length Discourses of the Buddha,* trans. by Bhikkhu Bodhi

There are many ways up the mountain, but each of us must choose a practice that feels true to his own heart. It is not necessary for you to evaluate the practices chosen by others. Remember, the practices themselves are only vehicles for you to develop awareness, lovingkindness, and compassion on the path toward freedom, a true freedom of spirit.

As the Buddha said, "One need not carry the raft on one's head after crossing the stream." We need to learn not only how to honor and use a practice for as long as it serves us—which in most cases is a very long time—but to look at it as just that, a vehicle, a raft to help us cross through the waters of doubt, confusion, desire, and fear. We can be thankful for the raft that supports our journey, and still realize that though we benefit, not everyone will take the same raft.

—Jack Kornfield, *A Path with Heart*

Perhaps Buddhism is the only religion that speaks about its own teachings as a raft to cross the river and not as an absolute truth to be worshipped and safeguarded. This is the most drastic measure that Buddhism utilizes to deal with dogmatism and fanaticism, which are the causes of so much conflict and violence. . . . According to Buddhism, knowledge itself can be an obstacle to true understanding, while views are a barrier to insight. Clinging to our views can cause us to lose the opportunity to come to a higher or more profound understanding of reality. Buddhism urges us to transcend our own knowledge in order to advance on the path to enlightenment. All views are considered to be "obstacles to knowledge." . . . According to Buddhist teaching, if we cannot continually expand the frontiers of our knowledge, we will be imprisoned by our own views and never able to attain the Way.

—Thich Nhat Hanh, *Interbeing*

When we study Buddhism, we learn abou
meditation as supports for encouraging us t
just be with things as they are. . . . These
likened to a raft. You need the raft to cross
the other side; when you get over there, yo
hind. That's an interesting image, but in e
like the raft gives out on you in the middle o
never really get to solid ground.

—Pema Chödrön, *Start Where You Are*

Spiritual practice is difficult in the beginning. You wonder how on earth you can ever do it. But as you get used to it, the practice gradually becomes easier. Do not be too stubborn or push yourself too hard. If you practice in accord with your individual capacity, little by little you will find more pleasure and joy in it. As you gain inner strength, your positive actions will gain in profundity and scope.

—The Dalai Lama, *A Flash of Lightning in the Dark of Night*

121. Do not think lightly of evil, saying: "It will not come to me." Even a water-pot is filled by the falling of drops. Likewise the fool, gathering it drop by drop, fills himself with evil.

122. Do not think lightly of good, saying: "It will not come to me." Even as a water-pot is filled by the falling of drops, so the wise man, gathering it drop by drop, fills himself with good.

—*The Dharmapada,* in Walpola Rahula's
What the Buddha Taught

During the student uprising in Burma, when the soldiers entered a temple to roust out dissidents, they would take off their shoes yet hold onto their guns. They were showing respect to the Buddha, while overlooking the dharma. It's essential to be accountable for our actions and not overlook the dharma in any domain.

—Sharon Salzberg, *Tricycle: The Buddhist Review,* Vol. II, #3

The Buddhist path is designed to reveal ever deeper levels of reality. We live in a pluralistic society. We live in a racist society, a homophobic and sexist society; in addition, Buddhists of every color, each gender, and all sexual orientations embrace the sectarian prejudices that developed in Asia. We live in a society that is pleading for us to put our shoulders to the wheel. We are also, each and every one of us, whole and perfect as is, interrelated, essentially non-separated, and equal. This, too, must be realized. If we forsake the inside for the outside, it is not just Buddhism that is diminished but the horizons for true social transformation as well.

—Helen Tworkov, *Tricyle: The Buddhist Review,* Vol. IV, #1

When I meet people in different parts of the world, I am always reminded that we are all basically alike: we are all human beings. Maybe we have different clothes, our skin is of a different color, or we speak different languages. This is on the surface. But basically, we are the same human beings. That is what binds us to each other. That is what makes it possible for us to understand each other and to develop friendship and closeness. . . . Because we all share this small planet earth, we have to learn to live in harmony and peace with each other and with nature. That is not just a dream, but a necessity.

—The Dalai Lama, "Nobel Peace Prize Lecture," in *The Dalai Lama: A Policy of Kindness,* edited by Sidney Piburn

To find a Buddha, you have to see your nature. Whoever sees his nature is a Buddha. If you don't see your nature, invoking Buddhas, reciting sutras, making offerings, and keeping precepts are all useless. Invoking Buddhas results in good karma, reciting sutras results in a good memory; keeping precepts results in a good rebirth, and making offerings results in future blessings—but no Buddha. . . .

To find a Buddha all you have to do is see your nature. Your nature is the Buddha. And the Buddha is the person who's free: free of plans, free of cares. If you don't see your nature and run around all day looking somewhere else, you'll never find a Buddha.

—*The Zen Teachings of Bodhidharma*

I wandered for alms.
I leaned on a stick.
My whole body was weak
and trembled.
Suddenly I fell down
and could see clearly
the misery of this body.
My heart was freed.

—Dhamma, in Susan Murcott's
The First Buddhist Women

We shield our heart with an armor woven out of very old habits of pushing away pain and grasping at pleasure. When we begin to breathe in the pain instead of pushing it away, we begin to open our hearts to what's unwanted. When we relate directly in this way to the unwanted areas of our lives, the airless room of ego begins to be ventilated.

—Pema Chödrön, *Start Where You Are*

I think of how some babies come screaming into the world, seem bad-tempered from the start, and how hard it is to hold a baby like that. Can I feel myself as the screaming baby, uncomfortable, dissatisfied? As the mother, frightened, irritated?

Can I catch my own irritation and fear and not run from it? Can I tolerate my own helplessness? Can I observe myself as I rush to defend my point of view with the same bullying tactics I condemn in "the other"? To the extent than I can see the soldier, the fundamentalist, the terrorist in me—view my own "stuff" and not separate from it—to that extent can I connect to "the other." It's the same stuff.

So with each breath, I confirm that the skinheads are my sons, the fundamentalists, me. And each time I do this, there's more space inside of me and I can allow more in. Their suffering, my suffering. In breath, out breath.

—Pat Enkyo O'Hara, *Tricycle: The Buddhist Review,* Vol. III, #4

The emperor of China asked a renowned Buddhist master if it would be possible to illustrate the nature of self in a visible way. In response, the master had a sixteen-sided room appointed with floor-to-ceiling mirrors that faced one another exactly. In the center he hung a candle aflame. When the emperor entered he could see the individual candle flame in thousands of forms, each of the mirrors extending it far into the distance. Then the master replaced the candle with a small crystal. The emperor could see the small crystal reflected again in every direction. When the master pointed closely at the crystal, the emperor could see the whole room of thousands of crystals reflected in each tiny facet of the crystal in the center. The master showed how the smallest particle contains the whole universe.

True emptiness is not empty, but contains all things. The mysterious and pregnant void creates and reflects all possibilities. From it arises our individuality, which can be discovered and developed, although never possessed or fixed. The self is held in no-self, as the candle flame is held in great emptiness.

—Jack Kornfield, *A Path with Heart*

If everything is impermanent, then everything is what we call "empty," which means lacking in any lasting, stable, and inherent existence; and all things, when seen and understood in their true relation, are not independent but interdependent with all other things. The Buddha compared the universe to a vast net woven of a countless variety of brilliant jewels, each with a countless number of facets. Each jewel reflects in itself every other jewel in the net and is, in fact, one with every other jewel.

Think of a wave in the sea. Seen in one way, it seems to have a distinct identity, an end and a beginning, a birth and a death. Seen in another way, the wave itself doesn't really exist but is just the behavior of water, "empty" of any separate identity but "full" of water. So when you really think about the wave, you come to realize that it is something made temporarily possible by wind and water, and is dependent on a set of constantly changing circumstances. You also realize that every wave is related to every other wave.

—Sogyal Rinpoche, *The Tibetan Book of Living and Dying*

When I realize that the question, "What is right livelihood?" arises out of the idea/feeling of being a separate entity with its inevitable feelings of insecurity, insufficiency, discontent, guilt, loneliness, fear, and wanting, doesn't it follow inevitably that I yearn for a livelihood that will compensate me for what I feel lacking and hurting inside? . . . When our habitual ideas and feelings of separation begin to abate in silent questioning, listening, and understanding, then right livelihood ceases to be a problem. Whatever we may be doing during the twenty-four hours a day, be it work for money or work for fun, service, leisure, creation or recreation, cleaning toilets, or nothing at all, the doing now, this moment of no separation, is the fulfillment, and it affects everyone and everything everywhere. Nothing else is more worthwhile. Everyone and everything is inextricably interweaving in this mysterious fabric called life.

—Toni Packer, in Claude Whitmyer's
Mindfulness and Meaningful Work

64. Although people work in order to be happy,
    It is uncertain whether or not they will find it;
    But how can those whose work itself is joy
    Find happiness unless they do it?

    —Shantideva, *A Guide to the Bodhisattva's Way of Life,*
    trans. by Stephen Batchelor

Awakening entails economic pursuits that foster self-respect and self-reliance and that serve to integrate, rather than disperse, the energies of the local community. From the perspective of the Dharma, economic goals include not only production and profit, but also their human and environmental impact. The conservation of material resources, their humane use, and their equitable distribution are taken as preeminent concerns.

—Joanna Macy, in Claude Whitmyer's
Mindfulness and Meaningful Work

The Sufis have a saying, "Praise Allah, and tie your camel to the post." This brings together both parts of practice: pray, yes, but also make sure you do what is necessary in the world. Have a life of meditation and genuine spiritual experience and, at the same time, discover how to manifest that here and now.

—Jack Kornfield, *Seeking the Heart of Wisdom*

The Buddha is a being who is totally free of all delusions and faults, who is endowed with all good qualities and has attained the wisdom eliminating the darkness of ignorance. The Dharma is the result of his enlightenment. After having achieved enlightenment, a Buddha teaches, and what he or she teaches is called the Dharma. The Sangha is made up of those who engage in the practice of the teachings given by the Buddha. . . .

One of the benefits of refuge is that all the misdeeds you have committed in the past can be purified, because taking refuge entails accepting the Buddha's guidance and following a path of virtuous action.

—The Dalai Lama, *The Way to Freedom*

When we trust with our open heart, whatever occurs, *at the very moment that it occurs,* can be perceived as fresh and unstained by the clouds of hope and fear. Chögyam Trungpa Rinpoche used the phrase "first thought, best thought" to refer to that first moment of fresh perception, before the colorful and coloring clouds of judgment and personal interpretation take over. "First thought" is "best thought" because it has not yet got covered over by all our opinions and interpretations, our hopes and fears, our likes and dislikes. It is direct perception of the world as it is. Sometimes we discover "first thought, best thought" by relaxing into the present moment in a very simple way.

—Jeremy Hayward, *Tricycle: The Buddhist Review,* Vol. IV, #3

Mindfulness is present-time awareness. It takes place in the here and now. It is the observance of what is happening right now, in the present moment. It stays forever in the present, perpetually on the crest of the ongoing wave of passing time. If you are remembering your second-grade teacher, that is memory. When you then become aware that you are remembering your second-grade teacher, that is mindfulness. If you then conceptualize the process and say to yourself, "Oh, I am remembering," that is thinking.

—Henepola Gunaratana, *Mindfulness in Plain English*

People often confuse meditation with prayer, devotion, or vision. They are not the same. Meditation as a practice does not address itself to a deity or present itself as an opportunity for revelation. This is not to say that people who are meditating do not occasionally think they have received a revelation or experienced visions. They do. But to those for whom meditation is their central practice, a vision or a revelation is seen as just another phenomenon of consciousness and as such is not to be taken as exceptional. The meditator would simply experience the ground of consciousness, and in doing so avoid excluding or excessively elevating any thought or feeling. To do this one must release all sense of the "I" as experiencer, even the "I" that might think it is privileged to communicate with the divine.

—Gary Snyder, *Tricycle: The Buddhist Review,* Vol. I, #1

When you dwell in stillness, the judging mind can come through like a foghorn. I don't like the pain in my knee. . . . This is boring. . . . I like this feeling of stillness; I had a good meditation yesterday, but today I'm having a bad meditation. . . . It's not working for me. I'm no good at this. I'm no good, period. This type of thinking dominates the mind and weighs it down. It's like carrying around a suitcase full of rocks on your head. It feels good to put it down. Imagine how it might feel to suspend all your judging and instead to let each moment be just as it is, without attempting to evaluate it as "good" or "bad." This would be a true stillness, a true liberation.

Meditation means cultivating a non-judging attitude toward what comes up in the mind, come what may.

—Jon Kabat-Zinn, *Wherever You Go, There You Are*

For a true spiritual transformation to flourish, we must see beyond [the] tendency to mental self-flagellation. Spirituality based on self-hatred can never sustain itself. Generosity coming from self-hatred becomes martyrdom. Morality born of self-hatred becomes rigid repression. Love for others without the foundation of love for ourselves becomes a loss of boundaries, codependency, and a painful and fruitless search for intimacy. But when we contact, through meditation, our true nature, we can allow others to also find theirs.

—Sharon Salzberg, *Lovingkindness*

If one desires to become a Buddhist, there is no initiation ceremony (or baptism) which one has to undergo. . . . If one understands the Buddha's teaching, and if one is convinced that his teaching is the right Path and if one tries to follow it, then one is a Buddhist. But according to the unbroken age-old tradition in Buddhist countries, one is considered a Buddhist if one takes the Buddha, the *Dhamma* (the Teaching) and the *Sangha* (the Order of Monks)—generally called "the Triple-Gem"—as one's refuges, and undertakes to observe the Five Precepts—the minimum moral obligations of a lay Buddhist—(1) not to destroy life, (2) not to steal, (3) not to commit adultery, (4) not to tell lies, (5) not to take intoxicating drinks. . . .

There are no external rites or ceremonies which a Buddhist has to perform. Buddhism is a way of life, and what is essential is following the Noble Eightfold Path. Of course there are in all Buddhist countries simple and beautiful ceremonies on religious occasions. . . . These traditional observances, though inessential, have their value in satisfying the religious emotions and needs of those who are less advanced intellectually and spiritually, and helping them gradually along the Path.

—Walpola Rahula, *What the Buddha Taught*

To take refuge in the Buddha means acknowledging the seed of enlightenment that is within ourselves, the possibility of freedom. It also means taking refuge in those qualities which the Buddha embodies, qualities like fearlessness, wisdom, love and compassion. Taking refuge in the Dharma means taking refuge in the law, in the way things are; it is acknowledging our surrender to the truth, allowing the Dharma to unfold within us. Taking refuge in the Sangha means taking support in the community, in all of us helping one another towards enlightenment and freedom.

—Joseph Goldstein, *The Experience of Insight*

To take refuge in the Buddha is to take refuge in someone who let go of holding back just as you can do. To take refuge in the dharma is to take refuge in all the teachings that encourage you and nurture your inherent ability to let go of holding back. And to take refuge in the sangha is to take refuge in the community of people who share this longing to let go and open rather than shield themselves. The support that we give each other as practitioners is not the usual kind of samsaric support in which we all join the same team and complain about someone else. It's more that you're on your own, completely alone, but it's helpful to know that there are forty other people who are also going through this all by themselves. That's very supportive and encouraging. Fundamentally, even though other people can give you support, you do it yourself, and that's how you grow up in this process, rather than becoming more dependent.

—Pema Chödrön, *Start Where You Are*

Taking refuge in the Buddha implies no personal guarantee that the Buddha himself will effect the arrival at the Goal of any of his followers. To the contrary, he says: "Surely by oneself is evil done, by oneself one becomes pure. Purity and impurity are of the individual. No one purifies another." . . . According to the doctrine of karma, future happiness is a direct result or continuation of the maintaining of a satisfactory standard of conduct in the present.

—Hammalawa Saddhatissa, *Buddhist Ethics*

A single act of giving has a value beyond what we can imagine. So much of the spiritual path is expressed and realized in giving: love, compassion, sympathetic joy, equanimity; letting go of grasping, aversion, and delusion. To give is powerful. That is why the Buddha said that if we knew, as he did, the power of giving, we would not let a single meal pass without sharing some of it.

Sharing food is a metaphor for all giving. When we offer someone food, we are not just giving that person something to eat; we are giving far more. We give strength, health, beauty, clarity of mind, and even life, because none of those things would be possible without food. So when we feed another, this is what we are offering: the substance of life itself.

—Sharon Salzberg, *Lovingkindness*

Enlightenment is like the moon reflected on the water. The moon does not get wet, nor is the water broken. Although its light is wide and great, the moon is reflected even in a puddle an inch wide. The whole moon and the entire sky are reflected in dewdrops on the grasses, or even in one drop of water.

Enlightenment does not divide you, just as the moon does not break the water. You cannot hinder enlightenment, just as a drop of water does not hinder the moon in the sky.

The depth of the drop is the height of the moon. Each reflection, however long or short its duration, manifests the vastness of the dewdrop, and realizes the limitlessness of the moonlight in the sky.

—Zen Master Dogen, *Moon in a Dewdrop*,
edited by Kazuaki Tanahashi

Dharma, a Sanskrit word for which there is no adequate English equivalent, refers to the understanding and behavior that lead to the elimination of suffering and its source and to the experience of a lasting state of happiness and fulfillment. . . . Shantideva, a seventh-century Indian Buddhist sage, writes:

> Although we wish to cast off grief,
> We hasten after misery;
> And though we long for happiness,
> Out of ignorance we crush our joy
> as if it were our enemy.

We wish for happiness, yet frequently we fail to identify its source. We wish to be free of suffering, frustration, and grief, but we do not correctly identify the sources of our unhappiness. So, although we wish to be free of misery we hasten after it, all the while destroying the causes of the happiness we could have.

—B. Alan Wallace, *Tibetan Buddhism from the Ground Up*

Suffering is a big word in Buddhist thought. It is a key term and it should be thoroughly understood. The Pali word is *dukkha*, and it does not just mean the agony of the body. It means that deep, subtle sense of unsatisfactoriness which is a part of every mind moment and which results directly from the mental treadmill. The essence of life is suffering, said the Buddha. At first glance this seems exceedingly morbid and pessimistic. It even seems untrue. After all, there are plenty of times when we are happy. Aren't there? No, there are not. It just seems that way. Take any moment when you feel really fulfilled and examine it closely. Down under the joy, you will find that subtle, all-pervasive undercurrent of tension, that no matter how great this moment is, it is going to end. No matter how much you just gained, you are either going to lose some of it or spend the rest of your days guarding what you have got and scheming how to get more. And in the end, you are going to die. In the end, you lose everything. It is all transitory.

—Henepola Gunaratana, *Mindfulness in Plain English*

Kisagotami was a poor widow who had suffered many cruel reversals in life. Then, a final twist of the knife, the beloved baby that was all she had in the world died. She was unconsolable and would not have the child's body cremated. Despairing, some of her fellow villagers suggested she go to see the Buddha. She arrived before him, still clutching the child's corpse in her arms. "Give me some special medicine that will cure my child," she begged.

The Buddha knew at once that the woman could not take the bald truth, so he thought for a while. Then he said, "Yes, I can help you. Go and get me three grains of mustard seed. But they have to come from a house in which no death has ever occurred."

Kisagotami set off with new hope in her heart. But as she went from door to door, she heard one heart-rending tale of bereavement after another. That evening, when she returned to the Buddha, she had learned that bereavement was not her own personal tragedy but a feature of the human condition—and she had accepted the fact.

Sadly, she laid down her dead child's body and bowed to the Buddha.

—John Snelling, *Elements of Buddhism*

The abandonment of religious virtue has left this culture aggressively antagonistic to the pursuit of the unknown, the unknowable, to the mystical realms of reality. The original enthusiasm for Zen in the United States was not just for personal discovery, but for the possibility of developing an appreciation for the unknown in an excessively cluttered society—it was an effort to break ground for new possibilities. What we need to know cannot arise from what we know now; our liberation from personal and collective suffering must derive from what we cannot envision, what is beyond our imagination, even beyond our dreams of what is possible.

One day an American student asked a Japanese Zen master, "Is enlightenment really possible?"

He answered. "If you're willing to allow for it."

—Helen Tworkov, *Tricyle: The Buddhist Review,* Vol III, #3

The true teaching is the kind of teaching that conforms to two things: First, it is consistent with the Buddhist insight. And secondly, it is appropriate for the person who is receiving it. It's like medicine. It has to be true medicine, and it must fit the person who is receiving it. Sometimes you can give someone a very expensive treatment, but they still die That is why when the Buddha meets someone and offers the teaching he has to know that person in order to be able to offer the appropriate teaching. Even if the teaching is very valuable, if you don't make it appropriate to the person, it is not Buddhist teaching.

—Thich Nhat Hanh, *Tricyle: The Buddhist Review,* Vol. IV, #4

Few people are capable of wholehearted commitment, and that is why so few people experience a real transformation through their spiritual practice. It is a matter of giving up our own viewpoints, of letting go of opinions and preconceived ideas, and instead following the Buddha's guidelines. Although this sounds simple, in practice most people find it extremely difficult. Their ingrained viewpoints, based on deductions derived from cultural and social norms, are in the way.

We must also remember that heart and mind need to work together. If we understand something rationally but don't love it, there is no completeness for us, no fulfillment. If we love something but don't understand it, the same applies. If we have a relationship with another person, and we love the person but don't understand him or her, the relationship is incomplete; if we understand the person but don't love him or her, it is equally unfulfilling. How much more so on our spiritual path. We have to understand the meaning of the teaching and also love it. In the beginning our understanding will only be partial, so our love has to be even greater.

—Ayya Khema, *When the Iron Eagle Flies*

I once heard a story about a visit to heaven and hell. In both places the visitor saw many people seated at a table on which many delicious foods were laid out. Chopsticks over a meter long were tied to their right hands, while their left hands were tied to their chairs. In hell, however much they stretched out their arms, the chopsticks were too long for them to get food into their mouths. They grew impatient and got their hands and chopsticks tangled with one another's. The delicacies were scattered here and there.

In heaven, on the other hand, people happily used the long chopsticks to pick out someone else's favorite food and feed it to him, and in turn they were being fed by others. They all enjoyed their meal in harmony.

—Shundo Aoyama, *Zen Seeds*

Intelligent practice always deals with just one thing: the fear at the base of human existence, the fear that *I am not*. And of course I am not, but the last thing I want to know is that. I am impermanence itself in a rapidly changing human form that appears solid. I fear to see what I am: an ever-changing energy field. I don't want to be that. So good practice is about fear. Fear takes the form of constantly thinking, speculating, analyzing, fantasizing. With all that activity we create a cloud cover to keep ourselves safe in make-believe practice. True practice is *not* safe; it's anything but safe. But we don't like that, so we obsess with our feverish efforts to achieve our version of the personal dream. Such obsessive practice is itself just another cloud between ourselves and reality. The only thing that matters is seeing with an impersonal searchlight: seeing things as they are. When the personal barrier drops away, why do we have to call it anything? We just live our lives. And when we die, we just die. No problem anywhere.

—Charlotte Joko Beck, *Everyday Zen*

The experience of the practice itself teaches us that any conception or ideal of awakened being can only be a hindrance—neither practice nor awakening is about our ideas or images. And yet, however limited the finger-pointing at the moon, still we point, we turn to one another for direction. So I have come to think that if the bodhisattva's task is to continue to practice until every pebble, every blade of grass, awakens, surely the passions, difficult or blissful, can also be included in that vow. And if awakening is also already present, inescapably and everywhere present from the beginning, how can the emotions not be part of that singing life of grasses and fish and oil tankers and subways and cats in heat who wake us, furious and smiling, in the middle of the brief summer night?

—Jane Hirshfield, *Tricycle: The Buddhist Review,* Vol. IV, #3

Whether people are beautiful and friendly or unattractive and disruptive, ultimately they are human beings, just like oneself. Like oneself, they want happiness and do not want suffering. Furthermore, their right to overcome suffering and be happy is equal to one's own. Now, when you recognize that all beings are equal in both their desire for happiness and their right to obtain it, you automatically feel empathy and closeness for them. Through accustoming your mind to this sense of universal altruism, you develop a feeling of responsibility for others: the wish to help them actively overcome their problems. Nor is this wish selective; it applies equally to all.

—The Dalai Lama, *Compassion and the Individual*

When you take photographs, just before you click the shutter, your mind is empty and open, just seeing without words. When you stand in front of a blank sheet of paper, about to make a painting or a calligraphy, you have no idea what you will do. Maybe you have some plan for a painting, or you know what symbol you want to calligraph, but you don't actually know what will appear when you put brush to paper. What you do out of trust in open mind will be fresh and spontaneous. Opening to first thought is the way to begin any action properly.

—Jeremy Hayward, *Tricycle: The Buddhist Review,* Vol. IV, #3

For 300 years after the Buddha's death there were no Buddha images. The people's practice was the image of the Buddha, there was no need to externalize it. But in time, as the practice was lost, people began to place the Buddha outside of their own minds, back in time and space. As the concept was externalized and images were made, great teachers started to reemphasize the other meaning of Buddha. There is a saying: "If you see the Buddha, kill him." Very shocking to people who offer incense and worship before an image. If you have a concept in the mind of a Buddha outside of yourself, kill it, let it go. . . . Gotama Buddha repeatedly reminded people that the experience of truth comes from one's own mind.

—Joseph Goldstein, *The Experience of Insight*

All our hand postures are mudras in that they are *associated* with subtle or not-so-subtle energies. Take the energy of the fist, for instance. When we get angry, our hands tend to close into fists. Some people unknowingly practice this mudra a lot in their lives. It waters the seeds of anger and violence within you every time you do it, and they respond by sprouting and growing stronger.

The next time you find yourself making fists out of anger, try to bring mindfulness to the inner attitude embodied in a fist. Feel the tension, the hatred, the anger, the aggression, and the fear which it *contains*. Then, in the midst of your anger, as an experiment, if the person you are angry at is present, try opening your fists and *placing* the palms together over your heart in the prayer position right in front of him. (Of course, he won't have the slightest idea what you are doing.) Notice what happens to the anger and hurt as you hold this position for even a few moments.

—Jon Kabat-Zinn, *Wherever You Go, There You Are*

Positive actions are difficult and infrequent. It is hard to have positive thoughts when our minds are influenced by emotions and confused by adverse circumstances. Negative thoughts arise by themselves, and it is rare that we do a positive action whose motivation, execution, and conclusion are perfectly pure. If our stock of hard-won positive actions is rendered powerless in an instant of anger, the loss is immeasurably more serious than that of some more abundant resource.

—The Dalai Lama, *Tricycle: The Buddhist Review,* Vol. II, #2

Shantideva emphasizes the importance of guarding our mind by drawing the following analogy:

> If a part of our body is wounded and we must walk through a jostling crowd, we shall be especially careful to guard and cover that wound. In a similar manner, when we are dwelling amongst harmful people or objects that cause our delusions to arise, we should guard the wound of our mind carefully.
>
> If we are anxious to protect an ordinary wound that can at most give us but a little temporary pain, then surely we should be highly motivated to guard the wound of our mind. If our mind remains unprotected and uncontrolled, it can lead us into hellish experiences of deep suffering and torment until we feel we are being crushed between two mighty mountains. [*Guide to a Bodhisattva's Way of Life*, 19–20]

—Geshe Kelsang Gyatso, *Meaningful to Behold*

In traditional Buddhist texts the five energies of Lust, Aversion, Torpor, Restlessness, and Doubt are called "Mind Hindrances" . . . because they obscure clear seeing, just as sandstorms in the desert or fog on a highway can cause travelers to get lost. They hinder the possibility of us reconnecting with the peaceful self that is our essential nature. They confuse us. We think they are real. We forget that our actual nature is not the passing storm. The passing storm is the passing storm. Our essence remains our essence all the time.

Five different energies seem like a limited menu, but they present themselves in an infinite variety of disguises. Ice cream sundaes are different from pizzas are different from sex, but fundamentally they are all objects of the lustful desire. . . . Grumbly mind is grumbly mind; sleepy mind is sleepy mind; restless mind is restless mind; doubtful mind is doubtful mind.

The fact that it's in the nature of minds for storms to arise and pass away is not a problem. . . . [It] helps in keeping the spirits up to remember that the weather is going to change. Our difficult mind states become a problem only if we believe they are going to go on forever.

—Sylvia Boorstein, *It's Easier Than You Think*

All of [the] hindrances—desire, anger, sloth and torpor, restlessness, doubt—are mental factors. They are not self, just impersonal factors functioning in their own way. A simile is given to illustrate the effect of these different obstructions in the mind. Imagine a pond of clear water. Sense desire is like the water becoming colored with pretty dyes. We become entranced with the beauty and intricacy of the color and so do not penetrate to the depths. Anger, ill will, aversion, is like boiling water. Water that is boiling is very turbulent. You can't see through to the bottom. This kind of turbulence in the mind, the violent reaction of hatred and aversion, is a great obstacle to understanding. Sloth and torpor is like the pond of water covered with algae, very dense. One cannot possibly penetrate to the bottom because you can't see through the algae. It is a very heavy mind. Restlessness and worry are like a pond when windswept. The surface of the water is agitated by strong winds. When influenced by restlessness and worry, insight becomes impossible because the mind is not centered or calm. Doubt is like the water when muddied; wisdom is obscured by murkiness and cloudiness.

—Joseph Goldstein, *The Experience of Insight*

We tend to be particularly unaware that we are thinking virtually all the time. The incessant stream of thoughts flowing through our minds leaves us very little respite for inner quiet. And we leave precious little room for ourselves anyway just to be, without having to run around doing things all the time. Our actions are all too frequently driven rather than undertaken in awareness, driven by those perfectly ordinary thoughts and impulses that run through the mind like a coursing river, if not a waterfall. We get caught up in the torrent and it winds up submerging our lives as it carries us to places we may not wish to go and may not even realize we are headed for.

Meditation means learning how to get out of this current, sit by its bank and listen to it, learn from it, and then use its energies to guide us rather than to tyrannize us. This process doesn't magically happen by itself. It takes energy. We call the effort to cultivate our ability to be in the present moment "practice" or "meditation practice."

—Jon Kabat-Zinn, *Wherever You Go, There You Are*

One finds that no matter how sincere one's intention to be attentive and aware, the mind rebels against such instructions and races off to indulge in all manner of distractions, memories and fantasies. . . . The comforting illusion of personal coherence and continuity is ripped away to expose only fragmentary islands of consciousness separated by yawning gulfs of unawareness. . . . The first step in this practice of mindful awareness is radical self-acceptance.

Such self-acceptance, however, does not operate in an ethical vacuum, where no moral assessment is made of one's emotional states. The training in mindful awareness is part of a Buddhist path with values and goals. Emotional states are evaluated according to whether they increase or decrease the potential for suffering. If an emotion, such as hatred or envy, is judged to be destructive, then it is simply recognized as such. It is neither expressed through violent thoughts, words or deeds, nor is it suppressed or denied as incompatible with a "spiritual" life. In seeing it for what it is—a transient emotional state—one mindfully observes it follow its own nature: to arise, abide for a while, and then pass away.

—Stephen Batchelor, *The Awakening of the West*

A sensation appears, and liking or disliking begins. This fleeting moment, if we are unaware of it, is repeated and intensified into craving and aversion, becoming a strong emotion that eventually overpowers the conscious mind. We become caught up in the emotion, and all our better judgment is swept aside. The result is that we find ourselves engaged in unwholesome speech and action, harming ourselves and others. We create misery for ourselves, suffering now and in the future, because of one moment of blind reaction.

But if we are aware at the point where the process of reaction begins—that is, if we are aware of the sensation—we can choose not to allow any reaction to occur or to intensify . . . in those moments the mind is free. Perhaps at first these may be only a few moments in a meditation period, and the rest of the time the mind remains submerged in the old habit of reaction to sensations, the old round of craving, aversion, and misery. But with repeated practice those few brief moments will become seconds, will become minutes, until finally the old habit of reaction is broken, and the mind remains continuously at peace. This is how suffering can be stopped.

—S. N. Goenka, *The Art of Living*

33. The mind is wavering and restless, difficult to guard and restrain: let the wise man straighten his mind as a maker of arrows makes his arrows straight.
34. Like a fish which is thrown on dry land, taken from his home in the waters, the mind strives and struggles to get free from the power of Death.
35. The mind is fickle and flighty, it flies after fancies wherever it likes: it is difficult indeed to restrain. But it is a great good to control the mind; a mind self-controlled is a source of great joy.

—*The Dhammapada,* trans. by Juan Mascaro

"Your arrows do not carry," observed the Master, "because they do not reach far enough spiritually. You must act as if the goal were infinitely far off. For master archers it is in fact common experience that a good archer can shoot further with a medium-strong bow than an unspiritual archer can with the strongest. It does not depend on the bow, but on the presence of mind, on the vitality and awareness with which you shoot. . . ."

—Eugen Herrigel, *Zen and the Art of Archery*

Mindfulness, or awareness, does not mean that you should think and be conscious "I am doing this" or "I am doing that." No. Just the contrary. The moment you think "I am doing this," you become self-conscious, and then you do not live in the action, but you live in the idea "I am," and consequently your work too is spoiled. You should forget yourself completely, and lose yourself in what you do. The moment a speaker becomes self-conscious and thinks "I am addressing an audience," his speech is disturbed and his trend of thought broken. But when he forgets himself in his speech, in his subject, then he is at his best, he speaks well and explains things clearly. All great work—artistic, poetic, intellectual or spiritual—is produced at those moments when its creators are lost completely in their actions, when they forget themselves altogether, and are free from self-consciousness.

—Walpola Rahula, *What the Buddha Taught*

Sometimes, the thought of "I" suddenly arises with great force. . . . The situation is like that of a rock or a tree seen protruding up from the peak of a hill on the horizon: From afar it may be mistaken for a human being. Yet the existence of a human in that rock or tree is only an illusion. On deeper investigation, no human being can be found in any of the individual pieces of the protruding entity, nor in its collection of parts, nor in any other aspect of it. Nothing in the protrusion can be said to be a valid basis for the name "human being."

Likewise, the solid "I" which seems to exist somewhere within the body and mind is merely an imputation. The body and mind are no more represented by the sense of "I" than is the protruding rock represented by the word "human." This "I" cannot be located anywhere within any individual piece of the body and mind, nor is it found within the body and mind as a collection, nor is there a place outside of these that could be considered to be a substantial basis of the object referred to by the name "I."

—The Second Dalai Lama (1475–1542), in Samuel Bercholz's *Entering the Stream*

If the basic project of mainstream Buddhist practice is to unmask the ego illusion for what it is, one of the main prongs of attack is directed against desire. Desire gets a very bad press in the Buddhist scriptures. It is a poison, a disease, a madness. There is no living in a body that is subject to desire, for it is like a blazing house.

Now, desire lives and grows by being indulged. When not indulged by the application of ethical restraint and awareness, on the other hand, it stabilizes and begins to diminish, though this is not an easy or comfortable process, for the old urges clamor for satisfaction for a long time.

This kind of practice cuts directly against the main currents of modern consumer society, where desire is energetically encouraged and refined to new pitches and variations by the powerful agencies of marketing and publicity. But it also cuts against the more moderate desires—for family, wealth, sense-pleasures and so on sanctioned in simpler, more traditional societies, including the one into which the Buddha was born. We can never be at peace while desire is nagging at us.

—John Snelling, *Elements of Buddhism*

That everything is included within your mind is the essence of mind. To experience this is to have religious feeling. Even though waves arise, the essence of your mind is pure; it is just like clear water with a few waves. Actually water always has waves. Waves are the practice of the water. To speak of waves apart from water or water apart from waves is a delusion. Water and waves are one. Big mind and small mind are one. When you understand your mind in this way, you have some security in your feeling. As your mind does not expect anything from outside, it is always filled. A mind with waves in it is not a disturbed mind, but actually an amplified one. Whatever you experience is an expression of big mind.

The activity of big mind is to amplify itself through various experiences. In one sense our experiences coming one by one are always fresh and new, but in another sense they are nothing but a continuous or repeated unfolding of the one big mind.

—Shunryu Suzuki, *Zen Mind, Beginner's Mind*

Each of us has a switching mechanism in our mind that allows us to move from one state of mind to another in an instant. . . . In fact, the surprising thing is not that we have the ability to switch our mind state, but that we have the ability to maintain a mind state, to continue a thought for more than an instant. Thoughts are constantly falling away, yet somehow we are able to maintain coherent ideas. Moreover, we have the facility to remember, which is a miraculous phenomenon if each and every moment the world is completely new. What is it that is remembering and what is there to remember? The image that the Buddhists use to work with this paradox is the idea of a flame being passed from candle to candle. We cannot say the flame is the same from one candle to the next, yet each is dependent upon the one just before it. Not only does this account for the potential transmission of thought but also for memory, because each flame has a quality of the original flame as far back as one wishes to travel.

—David A. Cooper, *Silence, Simplicity and Solitude*

Somewhere in this process, you will come face to face with the sudden and shocking realization that you are completely crazy. Your mind is a shrieking, gibbering madhouse on wheels barreling pell-mell down the hill, utterly out of control and hopeless. No problem. You are not crazier than you were yesterday. It has always been this way, and you just never noticed. You also are no crazier than anybody else around you. The real difference is that you have confronted the situation; they have not. So they still feel relatively comfortable. That does not mean that they are better off. Ignorance may be bliss, but it does not lead to Liberation. So don't let this realization unsettle you. It is a milestone actually, a sign of real progress. The very fact that you have looked at the problem straight in the eye means that you are on your way up and out of it.

—Henepola Gunaratana, *Mindfulness in Plain English*

We could become quite satisfied with ourselves because we are sitting in meditation and are endeavoring to practice the spiritual path. Such satisfaction with ourselves is not the same as contentment. Contentment is necessary, self-satisfaction is detrimental. To be content has to include knowing we are in the right place at the right time to facilitate our own growth. But to be self-satisfied means that we no longer realize the need for growth. All these aspects are important parts of our commitment and make us into one whole being with a one-pointed direction.

—Ayya Khema, *When the Iron Eagle Flies*

Responsibility does not only lie with the leaders of our countries or with those who have been appointed or elected to do a particular job. It lies with each of us individually. Peace, for example, starts within each one of us. When we have inner peace, we can be at peace with those around us. When our community is in a state of peace, it can share that peace with neighboring communities, and so on. When we feel love and kindness towards others, it not only makes others feel loved and cared for, but it helps us also to develop inner happiness and peace. And there are ways in which we can consciously work to develop feelings of love and kindness. For some of us, the most effective way to do so is through religious practice. For others it may be non-religious practices. What is important is that we each make a sincere effort to take seriously our responsibility for each other and for the natural environment.

—The Dalai Lama, "Nobel Peace Prize Lecture," in
The Dalai Lama: A Policy of Kindness,
edited by Sidney Piburn

Peace is a natural mind-state in every one of us. Peace has been there since the day we were born and it is going to be there till the day we die. It is our greatest gift; so why do we think we have no peace of mind?

Experiencing peace is like looking at our hands. Usually, we see only the fingers—not the spaces in between. In a similar manner, when we look at the mind, we are aware of the active states, such as our running thoughts and the one-thousand-and-one feelings that are associated with them, but we tend to overlook the intervals of peace between them. If one were to be unhappy or sad every minute of the twenty-four-hour day, what would happen to us? I guess we would all be in the mad house!

—Thynn Thynn, *Living Meditation, Living Insight*

There's an old koan about a monk who went to his master and said, "I'm a very angry person, and I want you to help me." The master said, "Show me your anger." The monk said, "Well, right now I'm not angry. I can't show it to you." And the master said, "Then obviously it's not you, since sometimes it's not even there." Who we are has many faces, but these faces are not who we are.

—Charlotte Joko Beck, *Everyday Zen*

Nothing ever changes in this world through hating the enemy. Nothing ever changes through aggression and hatred. So if it's pushing your buttons, whether it's Hitler or an abusive parent or an immoral war—Hitler was wrong, a parent who abuses a child is wrong—you have got to keep working with your own negativity, with those feelings that keep coming up inside you. We have also had the experience of seeing wrong being done when there is no confusion and no bewilderment and we just say, Stop it! No buttons have been pushed. It's just wrong, unaccompanied by righteous indignation. When I feel righteous indignation, I know that it has something to do with me. In order to be effective in stopping brutality on this planet you have to work with your own aggressions, with what has been triggered in you, so that you can communicate from the heart with the rapist, the abuser, the murderer.

—Pema Chödrön, *Tricycle: The Buddhist Review,* Vol. III, #1

Hatred is far worse than any ordinary enemy. Of course, ordinary enemies harm us: that is why we call them enemies. But the harm they do is not just in order to make us unhappy; it is also meant to be of some help to themselves or their friends. Hatred, the inner enemy, however, has no other function but to destroy our positive actions and make us unhappy. That is why Shantideva calls it "My foe, whose sole intention is to bring me sorrow." From the moment it first appears, it exists for the sole purpose of harming us. So we should confront it with all the means we have, maintain a peaceful state of mind, and avoid getting upset.

—The Dalai Lama, *Tricycle: The Buddhist Review*, Vol. II, #2

A way to discover intimacy with ourselves and all of life is to live with integrity, basing our lives on a vision of compassionate nonharming. When we dedicate ourselves to actions that do not hurt ourselves or others, our lives become all of a piece, a seamless garment with nothing separate or disconnected in the spiritual reality we discover.

In order to live with integrity, we must stop fragmenting and compartmentalizing our lives. Telling lies at work and then expecting great truths in meditation is nonsensical. Using our sexual energy in a way that harms ourselves or others, and then expecting to know transcendent love in another arena, is mindless. Every aspect of our lives is connected to every other aspect of our lives. This truth is the basis for an awakened life.

When we live with integrity, we further enhance intimacy with ourselves by being able to rejoice, taking active delight in our actions.

—Sharon Salzberg, *Lovingkindness*

The Buddha described his teaching as "going against the stream." The unflinching light of mindful awareness reveals the extent to which we are tossed along in the stream of past conditioning and habit. The moment we decide to stop and look at what is going on (like a swimmer suddenly changing course to swim upstream instead of downstream), we find ourselves battered by powerful currents we had never even suspected—precisely because until that moment we were largely living at their command.

—Stephen Batchelor, *The Awakening of the West*

Practicing Buddhism is about discovering ourselves to be in a great, flowing river of continuities. Just as our mother and father live inside us, so do generations upon generations of mothers and fathers before them. Part of our task is to discover how all our ancestors inform our lives—and the same holds true for all forms of life, for we have been shaped not only by human ancestors but also by the environments in which they lived.

—Joan Halifax, *Tricycle: The Buddhist Review,* Vol. I, #4

We can talk about "oneness" until the cows come home. But how do we actually separate ourselves from others? How? The pride out of which anger is born is what separates us. And the solution is a practice in which we experience this separating emotion as a definite bodily state. When we do, A Bigger Container is created.

What is created, what grows, is the amount of life I can hold without it upsetting me, dominating me. At first this space is quite restricted, then it's a bit bigger, and then it's bigger still. It need never cease to grow. And the enlightened state is that enormous and compassionate space. But as long as we live we find there is a limit to our container's size and it is at that point that we must practice. And how do we know where this cut-off point is? We are at that point when we feel any degree of upset, of anger. It's no mystery at all. And the strength of our practice is how big that container gets. . . . This practice of making A Bigger Container is essentially spiritual because it is essentially nothing at all. A Bigger Container isn't a thing; awareness is not a thing. . . .

—Charlotte Joko Beck, *Everyday Zen*

The present moment is the most profound and challenging teacher we will ever meet in our lives. It is a compassionate teacher, it extends to us no judgment, no censure, no measurement of success and failure. The present moment is a mirror, in its reflection we learn how to see. Learning how to look into this mirror without deluding ourselves is the source of all wisdom. In this mirror we see what contributes to the confusion and discord in our lives and what contributes to harmony and understanding. We see the relationship between pain and its cause on a moment-to-moment level, we see the bond between love and its source. We see what it is that connects us and what it is that alienates us.

—Christina Feldman and Jack Kornfield,
Stories of the Spirit, Stories of the Heart

When the Buddha confronted the question of identity on the night of his enlightenment, he came to the radical discovery that we do not exist as separate beings. He saw into the human tendency to identify with a limited sense of existence and discovered that this belief in an individual small self is a root illusion that causes suffering and removes us from the freedom and mystery of life. He described this as *interdependent arising,* the cyclical process of consciousness creating identity by entering form, responding to contact of the senses, then attaching to certain forms, feelings, desires, images, and actions to create a sense of self.

In teaching, the Buddha never spoke of humans as persons existing in some fixed or static way. Instead, he described us as a collection of five changing processes: the processes of the physical body, of feelings, of perceptions, of responses, and of the flow of consciousness that experiences them all. Our sense of self arises whenever we grasp at or identify with these patterns. The process of identification, of selecting patterns to call "I," "me," "myself," is subtle and usually hidden from our awareness.

—Jack Kornfield, *A Path with Heart*

Imagine a child sleeping next to its parents and dreaming it is being beaten or is painfully sick. The parents cannot help the child no matter how much it suffers, for no one can enter the dreaming mind of another. If the child could awaken itself, it could be freed of this suffering automatically. In the same way, one who realizes that his own Mind is Buddha frees himself instantly from the sufferings arising from [ignorance of the law of] ceaseless change of birth-and-death. If a Buddha could prevent it, do you think he would allow even one sentient being to fall into hell? Without Self-Realization one cannot understand such things as these.

—Bassui Tokusho Zenji, "Dharma Talk on One Mind," in
Daily Sutras

There is only one teacher. What is that teacher? Life itself. And of course each one of us is a manifestation of life; we couldn't be anything else. Now life happens to be both a severe and an endlessly kind teacher. It's the only authority that you need to trust. And this teacher, this authority, is everywhere. You don't have to go to some special place to find this incomparable teacher, you don't have to have some especially quiet or ideal situation: in fact, the messier it is, the better. The average office is a great place. The average home is perfect. Such places are pretty messy most of the time—we all know from firsthand experience! That is where the authority, the teacher is.

—Charlotte Joko Beck, *Everyday Zen*

If you pay attention for just five minutes, you know some very fundamental dharma: things change, nothing stays comfortable, sensations come and go quite impersonally, according to conditions, but not because of anything that you do or think you do. Changes come and go quite by themselves. In the first five minutes of paying attention, you learn that pleasant sensations lead to the desire that these sensations will stay and that unpleasant sensations lead to the hope that they will go away. And *both* the attraction and the aversion amount to tension in the mind. *Both* are uncomfortable. So in the first minutes, you get a big lesson about suffering: wanting things to be other than what they are. Such a tremendous amount of truth to be learned just closing your eyes and paying attention to bodily sensations.

—Sylvia Boorstein, *Tricycle: The Buddhist Review,* Vol. II, #1

If other people offer you advice, instead of thinking, What business is it of yours to be making suggestions? Respect what they have to say and consider yourself as the disciple of all beings.

—The Dalai Lama, *A Flash of Lightning in the Dark of Night*

[I]n India, I was living in a little hut, about six feet by seven feet. It had a canvas flap instead of a door. I was sitting on my bed meditating, and a cat wandered in and plopped down on my lap. I took the cat and tossed it out the door. Ten seconds later it was back on my lap. We got into a sort of dance, this cat and I. I would toss it out, and it would come back. I tossed it out because I was trying to meditate, to get enlightened. But the cat kept returning. I was getting more and more irritated, more and more annoyed with the persistence of the cat. Finally, after about a half-hour of this coming in and tossing out, I had to surrender. There was nothing else to do. There was no way to block off the door. I sat there, the cat came back in, and it got on my lap. But I did not do anything. I just let go. Thirty seconds later the cat got up and walked out. So you see, our teachers come in many forms.

—Joseph Goldstein, *Transforming the Mind, Healing the World*

If we open our eyes and look at the universe, we observe the sun and moon, and the stars on the sky; mountains, rivers, plants, animals, fishes, and birds on the earth. Cold and warmth come alternately; shine and rain change from time to time without ever reaching an end. Again, let us close our eyes and calmly reflect upon ourselves. From morning to evening, we are agitated by the feelings of pleasure and pain, love and hate; sometimes full of ambition and desire, sometimes called to the utmost excitement of reason and will. Thus the action of mind is like an endless issue of a spring of water. As the phenomena of the external world are various and marvelous, so is the internal attitude of human mind. Shall we ask for the explanation of these marvelous phenomena? . . . Why is the mind subjected to constant agitation? For these Buddhism offers only one explanation, namely, the law of cause and effect. . . .

—Soyen Shaku, *Tricycle: The Buddhist Review,* Vol. II, #4

The theory of karma should not be confused with so-called "moral justice" or "reward and punishment." The idea of moral justice, or reward and punishment, arises out of the conception of a supreme being, a God, who sits in judgment, who is a law-giver and who decides what is right and wrong. The term "justice" is ambiguous and dangerous, and in its name more harm than good is done to humanity. The theory of karma is the theory of cause and effect, of action and reaction; it is a natural law, which has nothing to do with the idea of justice or reward and punishment. Every volitional action produces its effects or results. If a good action produces good effects and a bad action bad effects, it is not justice, or reward, or punishment meted out by anybody or any power sitting in judgment on your action, but this is in virtue of its own nature, its own law. This is not difficult to understand. But what is difficult is that, according to the karma theory, the effects of a volitional action may continue to manifest themselves even in a life after death.

—Walpola Rahula, *What the Buddha Taught*

The difference between the eye and the mind as faculties is that the former senses the world of colors and visible forms, while the latter senses the world of ideas and thoughts and mental objects. We experience different fields of the world with different senses. We cannot hear colors, but we can see them. Nor can we see sounds, but we can hear them. . . . What of ideas and thoughts? They are also a part of the world. But they cannot be sensed, they cannot be conceived by the faculty of the eye, ear, nose, tongue or body. Yet they can be conceived by another faculty, which is mind. Now ideas and thoughts are not independent of the world experienced by these five physical sense faculties. In fact they depend on, and are conditioned by, physical experiences. Hence a person born blind cannot have ideas of color, except through the analogy of sounds or some other things experienced through his other faculties. Ideas and thoughts which form a part of the world are thus produced and conditioned by physical experiences and are conceived by the mind. Hence mind is considered a sense faculty or organ, like the eye or the ear.

—Walpola Rahula, *What the Buddha Taught*

The Buddha compared faith to a blind giant who meets up with a very sharp-eyed cripple, called wisdom. The blind giant, called faith, says to the sharp-eyed cripple, "I am very strong, but I can't see; you are very weak, but you have sharp eyes. Come and ride on my shoulders. Together we will go far." The Buddha never supported blind faith, but a balance between heart and mind, between wisdom and faith. The two together will go far. The saying that blind faith can move mountains unfortunately omits the fact that, being blind, faith doesn't know which mountain needs moving. That's where wisdom is essential, which means that a thorough understanding of the teaching is crucial.

—Ayya Khema, *When the Iron Eagle Flies*

The five spiritual faculties—faith, energy, mindfulness, concentration, and wisdom—are our greatest friends and allies on this journey of understanding. These qualities are most powerful when they are in balance. Faith needs to be balanced with wisdom, so that faith is not blind and wisdom is not shallow or hypocritical. When wisdom outstrips faith, we can develop a pattern where we know something, and even know it deeply from our experience, yet do not live it. Faith brings the quality of commitment to our understanding. Energy needs to be balanced with concentration; effort will bring lucidity, clarity, and energy to the mind, which concentration balances with calmness and depth. An unbalanced effort makes us restless and scattered, and too much concentration that is not energized comes close to torpor and sleep. Mindfulness is the factor that balances all these and is therefore always beneficial.

—Joseph Goldstein, *Seeking the Heart of Wisdom*

Recognizing the power of our minds means that even as unfortunate or terrible things happen to us, we can receive them in a more spacious and ultimately more enlightened way. The Buddha taught his students to develop a power of love so strong that the mind becomes like space that cannot be tainted. If someone throws paint, it is not the air that will change color. Space will not hold the paint; it will not grasp it in any way. Only the walls, the barriers to space, can be affected by the paint.

The Buddha taught his students to develop a power of love so strong that their minds become like a pure, flowing river that cannot be burned. No matter what kind of material is thrown into it, it will not burn. Many experiences—good, bad, and indifferent—are thrown into the flowing river of our lives, but we are not burned, owing to the power of the love in our hearts.

—Sharon Salzberg, *Lovingkindness*

The near-enemy of love is attachment. Attachment masquerades as love. It says, "I will love you if you will love me back." It is a kind of "businessman's" love. So we think, "I will love this person as long as he doesn't change. I will love that thing if it will be the way I want it." But this isn't love at all—it is attachment. There is a big difference between love, which allows and honors and appreciates, and attachment, which grasps and demands and aims to possess. When attachment becomes confused with love, it actually separates us from another person. We feel we need this other person in order to be happy. This quality of attachment also leads us to offer love only toward certain people, excluding others.

—Joseph Goldstein, *Seeking the Heart of Wisdom*

In Mahayana Buddhism in particular great emphasis is laid on realizing the union of wisdom and compassionate action. Human fulfillment is seen to lie in the *integration* of the inner and outer dimensions of life, *not* in transcendent wisdom or world-saving compassion alone.

As long as we remain delusively convinced of our egoic separation, then we remain cut off from the capacity to empathize fully with others. Such empathy is nothing other than the affective response to insight into the absence of egoic separation. For when the fiction of isolated selfhood is exposed, instead of a gaping mystical void we discover that our individual existence is rooted in relationship with the rest of life. For Thich Nhat Hanh, this is the realization of "interbeing"; for the Dalai Lama that of "universal responsibility": two ideas at the heart of contemporary Engaged Buddhism.

—Stephen Batchelor, *The Awakening of the West*

Practice can be stated very simply. It is moving from a life of hurting myself and others to a life of not hurting myself and others. That seems so simple—except when we substitute for real practice some idea that we should be different or better than we are, or that our lives should be different from the way they are. When we substitute our ideas about what *should* be (such notions as "I should not be angry or confused or unwilling") for our life as it truly is, then we're off base and our practice is barren.

—Charlotte Joko Beck, *Everyday Zen*

One day the Buddha held up a flower in front of an audience of 1,250 monks and nuns. He did not say anything for quite a long time. The audience was perfectly silent. Everyone seemed to be thinking hard, trying to see the meaning behind the Buddha's gesture. Then, suddenly, the Buddha smiled. He smiled because someone in the audience smiled at him and at the flower. . . . To me the meaning is quite simple. When someone holds up a flower and shows it to you, he wants you to see it. If you keep thinking, you miss the flower. The person who was not thinking, who was just himself, was able to encounter the flower in depth, and he smiled.

That is the problem of life. If we are not fully ourselves, truly in the present moment, we miss everything.

—Thich Nhat Hanh, *Peace Is Every Step*

"Beings are owners of their actions . . . heirs of their actions; they originate from their actions, are bound to their actions, have their actions as their refuge. It is action that distinguishes beings as inferior and superior."

—Culakammavibhanga Sutta, in *The Middle Length Discourses of the Buddha*, trans. by Bhikkhu Bodhi

When we throw a banana peel into the garbage, if we are mindful, we know that the peel will become compost and be reborn as a tomato or a lettuce salad in just a few months. But when we throw a plastic bag into the garbage, thanks to our awareness, we know that a plastic bag will not become a tomato or a salad very quickly. Some kinds of garbage need four or five hundred years to decompose. Nuclear waste needs a quarter of a million years before it stops being harmful and returns to the soil. Living in the present moment in an awakened way, looking after the present moment with all our heart, we will not do things which destroy the future. That is the most concrete way to do what is constructive for the future.

—Thich Nhat Hanh, *Our Appointment with Life*

All things reflect, interpenetrate, and indeed contain all other things. This is the organic nature of the universe, and is called mutual interdependence in classical Buddhism. Affinity and co-incidence are its surface manifestations . . . the other is no other than myself. This is the foundation of the precepts and the inspiration for genuine human behavior.

To acknowledge one's own dark side with a smile and to acknowledge the shining side of the other person with a smile—this is practice. Keeping the shining side of one's self always in view and holding fast to the dark side of the other—this is not practice.

—Robert Aitken, *Encouraging Words*

As to the cause of all suffering,
it has its root in greed and desire.
If greed and desire are wiped out,
it will have no place to dwell.
To wipe out all suffering—
this is called the third rule.
For the sake of this rule, the rule of extinction,
one practices the way.
And when one escapes from the bonds of suffering,
this is called attaining emancipation.
By what means can a person attain emancipation?
Separating oneself from falsehood and delusion—
this alone may be called emancipation.

—*The Lotus Sutra*, trans. by Burton Watson

The person that desires to have only pleasure and refuses pain expends an enormous amount of energy resisting life—and at the same time misses out enormously. He or she is on a self-defeating mission in any case, for just as we evade certain forms of suffering we inevitably fall victim to others. Underlying our glitzy modern consumer culture there is a deep spiritual under-nourishment and malaise that manifests all kinds of symptoms: nervous disorders, loneliness, alienation, purposelessness . . . So blanking out, running away, burying our heads in sand or videotape will take us nowhere in the long run. If we really want to solve our problems—and the world's problems, for they stem from the same roots—we must open up and accept the reality of suffering with full awareness, as it strikes us, physically, emotionally, mentally, spiritually, in the here-now. Then, strange as it may seem, we reap vast rewards. For suffering has its positive side. From it we derive the experience of depth: of the fullness of our humanity, This puts us fully in touch with other people and the rest of the Universe.

—John Snelling, *Elements of Buddhism*

Wisdom replaces ignorance in our minds when we realize that happiness does not lie in the accumulation of more and more pleasant feelings, that gratifying craving does not bring us a feeling of wholeness or completeness. It simply leads to more craving and more aversion. When we realize in our own experience that happiness comes not from reaching out but from letting go, not from seeking pleasurable experience but from opening in the moment to what is true, this transformation of understanding then frees the energy of compassion within us. Our minds are no longer bound up in pushing away pain or holding on to pleasure. Compassion becomes the natural response of an open heart.

—Joseph Goldstein, *Seeking the Heart of Wisdom*

The spacious mind has room for everything. It is like the space in a room, which is never harmed by what goes in and out of it. In fact, we say "the space in this room," but actually, the room is in the space, the whole building is in the space. When the building has gone, the space will still be there. The space surrounds the building, and right now we are containing space in a room. With this view we can develop a new perspective. We can see that there are walls creating the shape of the room and there is the space. Looking at it one way, the walls limit the space in the room. But looking at it another way, we see that space is limitless.

—Ajahn Sumedho, *Tricycle: The Buddhist Review,* Vol. V, #1

Sitting is essentially a simplified space. Our daily life is in constant movement: lots of things going on, lots of people talking, lots of events taking place. In the middle of that, it's very difficult to sense that we are in our life. When we simplify the situation, when we take away the externals and remove ourselves from the ringing phone, the television, the people who visit us, the dog who needs a walk, we get a chance—which is absolutely the most valuable thing there is—to face ourselves. Meditation is not about some state, but about the meditator. It's not about some activity or about fixing something. It's about ourselves. If we don't simplify the situation the chance of taking a good look at ourselves is very small—because what we tend to look at isn't ourselves but everything else. If something goes wrong, what do we look at? We look at what's going wrong. We're looking *out there* all the time, and not at ourselves.

—Charlotte Joko Beck, *Everyday Zen*

Even if your house is flooded or burnt to the ground, whatever the danger that threatens it, let it concern only the house. If there's a flood, don't let it flood your mind. If there's a fire, don't let it burn your heart, let it be merely the house, that which is external to you, that is flooded and burned. Allow the mind to let go of its attachments. The time is ripe.

—Ajahn Chah, in Samuel Bercholz's *Entering the Stream*

When we meditate, we're creating a situation in which there's a lot of space. That sounds good but actually it can be unnerving, because when there's a lot of space you can see very clearly: you've removed your veils, your shields, your armor, your dark glasses, your earplugs, your layers of mittens, your heavy boots. Finally you're standing, touching the earth, feeling the sun on your body, feeling its brightness, hearing all the noises without anything to dull the sound. You take off your nose plug, and maybe you're going to smell lovely fresh air or maybe you're in the middle of a garbage dump. Since meditation has this quality of bringing you very close to yourself and your experience, you tend to come up against your edge faster. It's not an edge that wasn't there before, but because things are so simplified and clear, you see it, and you see it vividly and clearly.

—Pema Chödrön, *Tricycle: The Buddhist Review,* Vol. I, #1

Anyone can build a house of wood and bricks, but the Buddha taught that that sort of home is not our real home, it's only nominally ours. It's a home in the world and it follows the ways of the world. Our real home is inner peace. An external material home may well be pretty but it is not very peaceful. There's this worry and then that, this anxiety and then that. So we say it's not our real home, it's external to us, sooner or later we'll have to give it up. It's not a place we can live in permanently because it doesn't truly belong to us, it's part of the world. Our body is the same, we take it to be self, to be "me" and "mine," but in fact it's not really so at all, it's another worldly home.

—Ajahn Chah, in Samuel Bercholz's *Entering the Stream*

The Buddha recommended that every person should remember every single day that we are not here for ever. It is a guest performance, which can be finished any time. We don't know when; we have no idea. We always think that we may have seventy-five or eighty years, but who knows? If we remember our vulnerability every single day, our lives will be imbued with the understanding that each moment counts and we will not be so concerned with the future. Now is the time to grow on the spiritual path. If we remember that, we will also have a different relationship to the people around us. They too can die at any moment, and we certainly wouldn't like that to happen at a time when we are not loving towards them. When we remember that, our practice connects to this moment and meditation improves because there is urgency behind it. We need to act now. We can only watch this one breath, not the next one.

—Ayya Khema, *When the Iron Eagle Flies*

Perhaps the deepest reason why we are afraid of death is because we do not know who we are. We believe in a personal, unique, and separate identity—but if we dare to examine it, we find that this identity depends entirely on an endless collection of things to prop it up: our name, our "biography," our partners, family, home, job, friends, credit cards . . . It is on their fragile and transient support that we rely for our security. So when they are all taken away, will we have any idea of who we really are?

Without our familiar props, we are faced with just ourselves, a person we do not know, an unnerving stranger with whom we have been living all the time but we never really wanted to meet. Isn't that why we have tried to fill every moment of time with noise and activity, however boring or trivial, to ensure that we are never left in silence with this stranger on our own?

—Sogyal Rinpoche, *The Tibetan Book of Living and Dying*

What good is meditating on patience
If you will not tolerate insult?
What use are sacrifices
If you do not overcome attachment and revulsion?
What good is giving alms
If you do not root out selfishness?
What good is governing a great monastery
If you do not regard all beings as your beloved parents?

—*The Life of Milarepa,* trans. by Lobsang P. Lhalunga

A young man named Sigala used to worship the six cardinal points of the heavens—east, south, west, north, nadir and zenith—in obeying and observing the last advice given him by his dying father. The Buddha told the young man that in the "noble discipline" of his teaching the six directions were different. According to his "noble discipline" the six directions were: east: parents; south: teachers; west: wife and children; north: friends, relatives and neighbors; nadir: servants, workers and employees; zenith: religious men.

"One should worship these six directions," said the Buddha. Here the word "worship" is very significant, for one worships something sacred, something worthy of honor and respect. These six family and social groups mentioned above are treated in Buddhism as sacred, worthy of respect and worship. But how is one to "worship" them? The Buddha says that one could "worship" them only by performing one's duties toward them.

—Walpola Rahula, *What the Buddha Taught*

Shakyamuni Buddha's revolution was without warfare; without provoking violent opposition, he defied prevalent Brahmanic conventions to teach not only rulers and wealthy merchants but outcasts, the disinherited, street punks, even—eventually—women. He then went on to guide his diverse followers on the path of liberation. In the Buddha's teachings, the source of absolute liberation is internal, a state of mind that is not dependent on external circumstances—not on race, class, or gender. In dharma, democracy is the birthright of our own Buddha-nature, the democracy of being that goes beyond all culture, all concepts.

—Helen Tworkov, *Tricyle: The Buddhist Review,* Vol. IV, #1

If we take a motor car, we feel quite sure about what we have . . . until we start taking it apart. But once we have . . . taken out the gearbox and transmission, removed the wheels and so on—what's left? We don't have a car any more, just a set of spare parts.

It is the same with a person. That too can be stripped down to its basic components . . . the so-called skandhas or "groups." There is 1. the category of the physical, which includes the body and its five senses; 2. that of feeling; 3. perception; 4. mental formations (impulses and emotions); and 5. consciousness or mind. When these groups of components come together in proper working order, the right conditions exist for the illusion of a self and a person to arise. But once they break down and go their separate ways—as at physical death, for instance—then that self or person cannot be found.

—John Snelling, *Elements of Buddhism*

It is helpful in learning to appreciate and develop your ability to change to think about how you have changed over time. You are not the same person you were ten years ago. How are you different? What were you like before? Would your present self and past self be friends if they met? What would they like and dislike about each other? How did you come to be the person you are now? Your ideals, thoughts, and opinions have changed; what has replaced the old ones and why? By reviewing the changes that have occurred, you can savor the growth and progress you have made, and appreciate the benefits the process of change has brought to your life.

When you notice how much you have changed and developed even without consciously trying, you can see how much you could grow if you made a real effort to change.

—Tarthang Tulku, *Skillful Means*

We humans have existed in our present form for about a hundred thousand years. I believe that if during this time the human mind had been primarily controlled by anger and hatred, our overall population would have decreased. But today, despite all our wars, we find that the human population is greater than ever. This clearly indicates to me that love and compassion predominate in the world. And this is why unpleasant events are "news"; compassionate activities are so much a part of daily life that they are taken for granted and, therefore, largely ignored.

—The Dalai Lama, *Compassion and the Individual*

Tanzan and Ekido were once traveling together down a muddy road. A heavy rain was still falling. Coming around a bend, they met a lovely girl in a silk kimono and sash, unable to cross the intersection.

"Come on, girl," said Tanzan at once. Lifting her in his arms, he carried her over the mud.

Ekido did not speak again until that night when they reached a lodging temple. Then he no longer could restrain himself. "We monks don't go near females," he told Tanzan, "especially not young and lovely ones. It is dangerous. Why did you do that?"

"I left the girl there," said Tanzan. "Are you still carrying her?"

—Paul Reps, *Zen Flesh, Zen Bones*

Right livelihood is not just a philosophical ideal. It is a practical, achievable reality. Finding and maintaining right livelihood does require regular, consistent action, but the steps are clear and the results immediate. Finding your own right livelihood depends primarily on getting in touch with your "beginner's mind." Mindfulness challenges us to stay with things as they are and to change our lives through action that harms no one. Working together, mindfully and compassionately, we can create a community in which all our livelihoods are "right."

—Claude Whitmyer, *Mindfulness and Meaningful Work*

Right Livelihood appears to be harder to practice these days than in the time of the Buddha. The rule is still the same: Right Livelihood is organizing one's financial support so that it is nonabusive, nonexploitive, nonharming. However, these days what is abusive and exploitive is not necessarily self-evident.

When the Buddha taught, unwholesome livelihood categories were easy to distinguish. Soldiering, keeping slaves, manufacturing weapons and intoxicants—all were on the proscribed list. In our time, soldiers sometimes serve as peacekeepers. It's hard to know the wholesomeness of all the products of any corporation, corporate mergers being what they are. Who knows what else is being manufactured by my detergent company's subsidiaries? . . .

For me, a complete picture of wholesome Right Livelihood is even larger than the proscriptions that reflect *external choices*. Wholesome internal choices—healthy attitudes about one's work—also contribute to mental happiness and peace of mind. Everyone's livelihood is an opportunity for self-esteem.

—Sylvia Boorstein, *It's Easier Than You Think*

Those of us who start on the path to right livelihood find that our lives are more balanced, simple, clear, and focused. We are no longer strung out in a meaningless cycle of material consumption.

The contemporary economy focuses on this cycle of consumption. It doesn't really support our efforts to find meaningful work. Today, work is a means to consume or to pay debt for consumption already indulged in. How many people do you know who really love the work they are doing? How many feel bored and alienated? How many are simply earning the money to spend it on material pleasures?

Right livelihood demands that you take responsibility for making your work more meaningful. Good work is dignified. It develops your faculties and serves your community. It is a central human activity.

—Roger Pritchard, in Claude Whitmyer's
Mindfulness and Meaningful Work

If we do a little of one kind of practice and a little of another, the work we have done in one often doesn't continue to build as we change to the next. It is as if we were to dig many shallow wells instead of one deep one. In continually moving from one approach to another, we are never forced to face our own boredom, impatience, and fears. We are never brought face to face with ourselves. So we need to choose a way of practice that is deep and ancient and connected with our hearts, and then make a commitment to follow it as long as it takes to transform ourselves.

—Jack Kornfield, *A Path with Heart*

Devotion, scholarship, and meditation can all be empty rituals, and whether these devotional acts or any other practices are in fact Dharma depends solely upon one's motivation. . . . Our initial attempts at spiritual practice tend to be very self-conscious. We want to overcome the distortions of our minds and cultivate such wholesome qualities as kindness, insight, mindfulness, and concentration; but as we engage in practices designed to cultivate these, at first they appear to be only mental exercises. Dharma seems separate, something adopted from outside. But as we go deeper into the practice, this sense of separation begins to disappear; our minds become the very Dharma we seek to cultivate.

—B. Alan Wallace, *Tibetan Buddhism from the Ground Up*

Some people do not know the difference between "mindfulness" and "concentration." They concentrate on what they're doing, thinking that is being mindful. . . . We can concentrate on what we are doing, but if we are not mindful at the same time, with the ability to reflect on the moment, then if somebody interferes with our concentration, we may blow up, get carried away by anger at being frustrated. If we are mindful, we are aware of the tendency to first concentrate and then to feel anger when something interferes with that concentration. With mindfulness we can concentrate when it is appropriate to do so and not concentrate when it is appropriate not to do so.

—Ajahn Sumedho, *Teachings of a Buddhist Monk*

Awareness cannot be practiced.

There has been some confusion between awareness and mindfulness. They are related, but distinct. *Sati,* or mindfulness, implies there is action of the mind. We purposely set ourselves to pay attention to our minds. We exert effort. Awareness is different.

Awareness is devoid of any action.

The mind simply "awares." There is no action here, only a collected and spontaneous awareness that just "sees." Here, mindfulness is the cause, and awareness is the effect. You cannot practice or train the effect. You can only practice something that will cause it. We have to start with mindfulness so that awareness may arise in us.

—Thynn Thynn, *Living Meditation, Living Insight*

The Buddha always told his disciples not to waste their time and energy in metaphysical speculation. Whenever he was asked a metaphysical question, he remained silent. Instead, he directed his disciples toward practical efforts. Questioned one day about the problem of the infinity of the world, the Buddha said, "Whether the world is finite or infinite, limited or unlimited, the problem of your liberation remains the same." Another time he said, "Suppose a man is struck by a poisoned arrow and the doctor wishes to take out the arrow immediately. Suppose the man does not want the arrow removed until he knows who shot it, his age, his parents, and why he shot it. What would happen? If he were to wait until all these questions have been answered, the man might die first." Life is so short. It must not be spent in endless metaphysical speculation that does not bring us any closer to the truth.

—Thich Nhat Hanh, *Zen Keys*

We must have beginner's mind, free from possessing anything, a mind that knows everything is in flowing change. Nothing exists but momentarily in its present form and color. One thing flows into another and cannot be grasped. Before the rain stops we hear a bird. Even under the heavy snow we see snowdrops and some new growth. In the East I saw rhubarb already. In Japan in the spring we eat cucumbers.

—Shunryu Suzuki, *Zen Mind, Beginner's Mind*

In a dream you may stray and lose your way home. You ask someone to show you how to return or you pray to God or Buddhas to help you, but still you can't get home. Once you rouse yourself from your dream-state, however, you find that you are in your own bed and realize that the only way you could have gotten home was to awaken yourself. This [kind of spiritual awakening] is called "return to the origin" or "rebirth in paradise." It is the kind of inner realization that can be achieved with some training. . . . You would be making a serious error, however, were you to assume that this was true enlightenment in which there is no doubt about the nature of reality. You would be like a man who having found copper gives up the desire for gold.

—Bassui Tokusho Zenji, "Dharma Talk on One Mind," in
Daily Sutras

One day Mara, the Buddhist god of ignorance and evil, was traveling through the villages of India with his attendants. He saw a man doing walking meditation whose face was lit up in wonder. The man had just discovered something on the ground in front of him. Mara's attendants asked what that was and Mara replied, "A piece of truth." "Doesn't this bother you when someone finds a piece of the truth, o evil one?" his attendants asked. "No," Mara replied. "Right after this they usually make a belief out of it."

—Christina Feldman and Jack Kornfield,
Stories of the Spirit, Stories of the Heart

Do not think that time merely flies away. Do not see flying away as the only function of time. If time merely flies away, you would be separated from time. The reason you do not clearly understand the time-being is that you think of time only as passing.

In essence, all things in the entire world are linked with one another as moments. Because all moments are the time-being, they are your time-being.

The time-being has the quality of flowing. . . .

You may suppose that time is only passing away, and not understand that time never arrives. Although understanding itself is time, understanding does not depend on its own arrival.

People only see time's coming and going, and do not thoroughly understand that the time-being abides in each moment.

—Zen Master Dogen, *Moon in a Dewdrop,*
edited by Kazuaki Tanahashi

The first step . . . is to cut off the chain of associated concepts and words that flood the mind, holding it with recollection on the present, on what is. Thus in a famous verse, the Buddha used to say,

> Don't chase after the past,
> Don't seek the future;
> The past is gone
> The future hasn't come
> But see clearly on the spot
> That object which *is now,*
> While finding and living in
> A still, unmoving state of mind.

—Bhikkhu Mangalo, *The Practice of Recollection*

The Buddha stressed the dynamic nature of existence. This resonates with the ideas of some early Greek philosophers, such as Heraclitus, who maintained that "All is flux" and "You can't step into the same river twice."

Now, all this sounds like common sense. Yet there is something about our minds and emotions that kicks against the idea of change. We are forever trying to break the dynamic world-dance, which is a unity, into separate "things," which we then freeze in the ice of thought. But the world-dance doggedly refuses to remain fragmented and frozen. It swirls on, changing from moment to moment, laughing at all our pitiful attempts to organize and control it.

In order to live skillfully, in harmony with the dynamic Universe, it is essential to accept the reality of change and impermanence. The wise person therefore travels lightly, with a minimum of clutter, maintaining the proverbial "open mind" in all situations, for he or she knows that tomorrow's reality will not be the same as today's. He or she will also have learned the divine art of letting go—which means not being attached to people and possessions and situations, but rather, when the time for parting comes, allowing that to happen graciously.

—John Snelling, *Elements of Buddhism*

Nan-in, a Japanese master during the Meiji era (1868–1912), received a university professor who came to inquire about Zen.

Nan-in served tea. He poured his visitor's cup full and then kept on pouring. The professor watched the cup overflow until he no longer could restrain himself.

"It is overfull. No more will go in."

"Like this cup," Nan-in said, "you are full of your own opinions and speculations. How can I show you Zen unless you first empty your cup?"

—Paul Reps, *Zen Flesh, Zen Bones*

If I am holding a cup of water and I ask you, "Is this cup empty?" you will say, "No, it is full of water." But if I pour out the water and ask you again, you may say, "Yes, it is empty." But, empty of what? . . . My cup is empty of water, but it is not empty of air. To be empty is to be *empty of something*. . . . When Avalokita [Avalokiteshvara, the bodhisattva of compassion] says that the five skandhas are equally empty, to help him be precise we must ask, "Mr. Avalokita, empty of what?"

The five skandhas, which may be translated into English as five heaps, or five aggregates, are the five elements that comprise a human being. . . . In fact, these are really five rivers flowing together in us: the river of form, which means our body, the river of feelings, the river of perceptions, the river of mental formations, and the river of consciousness. They are always flowing in us. . . .

Avalokita looked deeply into the five skandhas . . . and he discovered that none of them can be by itself alone. . . . Form is empty of a separate self, but it is full of everything in the cosmos. The same is true with feelings, perceptions, mental formations, and consciousness.

—Thich Nhat Hanh, *The Heart of Understanding*

"There is no material that exists for the production of Name and Form; and when Name and Form cease, they do not go anywhither in space. After Name and Form have ceased, they do not exist anywhere in the shape of heaped-up music material. Thus when a lute is played upon, there is no previous store of sound; and when the music ceases it does not go anywhither in space. When it has ceased, it exists nowhere in a stored-up state. Having previously been non-existent, it came into existence on account of the structure and stem of the lute and the exertions of the performer; and as it came into existence so it passes away. In exactly the same way, all the elements of being, both corporeal and non-corporeal come into existence after having previously been non-existent; and having come into existence pass away."

—Paul Carus, *The Gospel of Buddha*

In a classical text entitled "The Questions of King Milinda," a monk named Nagasena uses an allegory . . . A group of people gathered on the edge of a flooding stream want to go to the far shore but are afraid. They don't know what to do until one wise person comes along, assesses the situation, takes a running leap and jumps to the other side. Seeing the example of that person, the others say, "Yes, it can be done." Then they also jump. In this story the near shore is our usual confused condition, and the far shore is the awakened mind. Inspired by witnessing another, we say, "Yes, it can be done." That is one level of faith. After we have jumped ourselves, when we say, "Yes, it can be done," that is quite another level of faith.

—Sharon Salzberg, *Tricycle: The Buddhist Review,* Vol. VI, #3

Garbage can smell terrible, especially rotting organic matter. But it can also become rich compost for fertilizing the garden. The fragrant rose and the stinking garbage are two sides of the same existence. Without one, the other cannot be. Everything is in transformation. The rose that wilts after six days will become a part of the garbage. After six months the garbage is transformed into a rose. When we speak of impermanence, we understand that everything is in transformation. This becomes that, and that becomes this.

Looking deeply, we can contemplate one thing and see everything else in it. We are not disturbed by change when we see the interconnectedness and continuity of all things. It is not that the life of any individual is permanent, but that life itself continues.

—Thich Nhat Hanh, *Present Moment, Wonderful Moment*

Modern culture would have us worship before the altar of the thinking mind, with its endless capacity to produce ideas, fantasies, and formulas. We are taught that the thinking mind is the possessor of all wisdom, and we dedicate much of our lives to the pursuit of knowledge and information. Seeing the world and ourselves through the filter of all the information we have accumulated, we can become imprisoned by the very ideas and images we have so ardently pursued. Often we think that we know ourselves, when what we know is only what we think about ourselves. When we think we know the world around us, our static images bar us from seeing the mystery held within each changing moment.

What is an image if not just a description of the world that is bound to the past?

—Christina Feldman and Jack Kornfield,
Stories of the Spirit, Stories of the Heart

There is a famous saying: "If the mind is not contrived, it is spontaneously blissful, just as water, when not agitated, is by nature transparent and clear." I often compare the mind in meditation to a jar of muddy water: The more we leave the water without interfering or stirring it, the more the particles of dirt will sink to the bottom, letting the natural clarity of the water shine through. The very nature of the mind is such that if you only leave it in its unaltered and natural state, it will find its true nature, which is bliss and clarity

So take care not to impose anything on the mind, or to tax it. When you meditate there should be no effort to control, and no attempt to be peaceful. Don't be overly solemn or feel that you are taking part in some special ritual; let go even of the idea that you are meditating. Let your body remain as it is, and your breath as you find it. Think of yourself as the sky, holding the whole universe.

—Sogyal Rinpoche, *The Tibetan Book of Living and Dying*

One of the most common analogies used to describe the Buddha-nature is space itself. This analogy has three aspects. First, just as space is omnipresent and yet is unpolluted by everything it pervades, similarly, Buddha-nature pervades every sentient being without being in any way tainted. Second, just as galaxies and universes arise and pass within space, so do the characteristics of our personalities arise and pass within Buddha-nature. Our sensations arise and pass away; Buddha-nature continues. Third, just as space is never consumed by fire, so this Buddha-nature is never consumed by the "fire" of aging, sickness, or death.

—B. Alan Wallace, *Tibetan Buddhism from the Ground Up*

The oft-cited parable of the burning house tells of a father distraught as his children blithely play, unaware that the house is ablaze. Knowing of their respective predilections for playthings, he lures them from the inferno with the promise that he has a cart for each waiting outside, a deer-drawn cart for one, a goat-drawn cart for another, and so on. When they emerge from the conflagration, they find only one cart, a magnificent conveyance drawn by a great white ox, something that they had never even dreamed of. The burning house is samsara, the children are ignorant sentient beings, unaware of the dangers of their abode, the father is the Buddha, who lures them out of samsara with the teaching of a variety of vehicles . . . knowing that in fact there is but one vehicle, the buddha vehicle whereby all beings will be conveyed to unsurpassed enlightenment.

—Donald S. Lopez, Jr., *Buddhism in Practice*

Shunryu Suzuki Roshi (1904–1971), founder of Zen Center San Francisco and author of *Zen Mind, Beginner's Mind,* was known to discourage questions about enlightenment. Once, when pressed on the subject, he replied:

"What do you want to know for? You may not like it."

—Suzuki Roshi, *Tricycle: The Buddhist Review,* Vol. VI, #3

Enlightening beings are like lotus flowers,
With roots of kindness, stems of peace,
Petals of wisdom,
Fragrance of conduct.

Enlightening beings turn the wheel of teaching
Just like what the buddhas turn;
Conduct is its hub, concentration the spokes;
Knowledge is their adornment, wisdom is their sword.

—*The Flower Ornament Scripture,*
trans. by Thomas Cleary

49. As the bee takes the essence of a flower and flies away without destroying its beauty and perfume, so let the sage wander in this life. . . .

54. The perfume of flowers goes not against the wind, not even the perfume of sandalwood, of rose-bay, or of jasmine; but the perfume of virtue travels against the wind and reaches unto the ends of the world. . . .

58. Even as on a heap of rubbish thrown away by the side of the road a lotus flower may grow and blossom with its pure perfume giving joy to the soul, in the same way among the blind multitudes shines pure the light of wisdom of the student who follows the Buddha, the one who is truly awake.

—*The Dhammapada,* trans. by Juan Mascaro

In early times in Japan, bamboo-and-paper lanterns were used with candles inside. A blind man, visiting a friend one night, was offered a lantern to carry home with him.

"I do not need a lantern," he said. "Darkness or light is all the same to me."

"I know you do not need a lantern to find your way," his friend replied, "but if you don't have one, someone else may run into you. So you must take it."

The blind man started off with the lantern and before he had walked very far someone ran squarely into him. "Look out where you are going!" he exclaimed to the stranger. "Can't you see this lantern?"

"Your candle has burned out, brother," replied the stranger.

—Paul Reps, *Zen Flesh, Zen Bones*

The hallmark of the enlightenment process is in being "here" and not "there." Indeed, the focal point of continuity is in being here at all times. The famous message of Ram Dass to "Be here now" is what results when one is adept in this practice. It is laborious in that it requires great perseverance—we are up against lifelong patterns—but it is a major enlightenment practice because it can break through our basic conditioning.

The secret of success in continuity practice is to eliminate any sense of failure. From the moment we begin, we are successful. The only measure of success is this moment, right now. Are we here? If we are here, our practice is perfect.

The fact that we have just returned from out yonder, or that we might take off again in a few seconds, is not relevant. Without this practice, we would always be spaced out. We would rarely experience being here. Thus, each moment we are able to break the pattern, we have succeeded.

—David A. Cooper, *Silence, Simplicity and Solitude*

The secret of beginning a life of deep awareness and sensitivity lies in our willingness to pay attention. Our growth as conscious, awake human beings is marked not so much by grand gestures and visible renunciations as by extending loving attention to the minutest particulars of our lives. Every relationship, every thought, every gesture is blessed with meaning through the wholehearted attention we bring to it.

In the complexities of our minds and lives we easily forget the power of attention, yet without attention we live only on the surface of existence. It is just simple attention that allows us truly to listen to the song of a bird, to see deeply the glory of an autumn leaf, to touch the heart of another and be touched. We need to be fully present in order to love a single thing wholeheartedly. We need to be fully awake in this moment if we are to receive and respond to the learning inherent in it.

—Christina Feldman and Jack Kornfield,
Stories of the Spirit, Stories of the Heart

What one thinks or reads is always qualified by the preposition "of," or "about," and does not give us the thing itself. Not mere talk about water, nor the mere sight of a spring, but an actual mouthful of it gives the thirsty complete satisfaction.

—D. T. Suzuki, *Essays in Zen Buddhism*

It will be a wholesome practice to remind oneself often of the fact that one's deeds, words, and thoughts first of all act upon and alter one's own mind. Reflecting thus will give a strong impetus to true self-respect which is preserved by protecting oneself against everything mean and evil. To do so will also open a new, practical understanding of a profound saying of the Buddha:

In this fathom-long body with its perceptions and thoughts there is the world, the origin of the world, the ending of the world and the path to the ending of the world. [*Anguttara Nikaya,* 4: 451]

—Nyanaponika Thera, *The Heart of Buddhist Meditation*

Adolf Hitler was a vegetarian; the Dalai Lama, the embodiment of compassion, eats meat by his doctors' orders. Clearly, there's more to mind than what is put into the mouth: yet, as long as food remains a fundamental part of life, these choices are a proper focus of spiritual awareness. Every bite of macaroni contains choices about culture, history, meaning—even the "Nutrition Facts" newly listed on every U.S. noodle box have resonances for us that spread as far as asceticism, sin, compassion, the place of science in our beliefs, and the importance of supporting one's own well-being along with that of others.

So what should a Buddhist eat?

—Kate Wheeler, *Tricycle: The Buddhist Review,* Vol. IV, #2

This exchange is probably the most famous in Zen lore. Bodhidharma met the emperor of the Liang Dynasty, a devout Buddhist renowned for his piety and charity, who was much given to endowing monasteries and orphanages. Wu said: "I have endowed temples and authorized ordinations—what is my merit?" Bodhidharma's answer was radical: "No merit at all." Wu had been doing good for the sake of accumulating merit. Bodhidharma cut through Wu's ideas about merit to the core of his teaching, that your practice isn't apart from you: when your mind is pure, you live in a pure universe; when you're caught up in ideas of gaining and losing, you live in a world of delusion.

—Jisho Cary Warner, *Tricycle: The Buddhist Review,* Vol. III, #3

It is a characteristic tendency of human beings to indulge in emotions such as happiness, grief, or anger in response to present conditions, failing to balance these feelings with the awareness that present conditions are results of past causes. It is illogical to face the present only as an object of enjoyment or tolerance, neglecting to use it as the opportunity to create the future.

—Muso Kokushi, *Dream Conversations*

The chief objects of refuge in Buddhist practice are the Buddha, the Dharma, or spiritual path that he revealed, and the Sangha, or spiritual community. . . . Taking refuge in these "Three Jewels" is to place our trust in them, confident they will not mislead us. This step does not entail a blind leap of faith, nor does it require a complete understanding of the qualities of the Three Jewels.

Generally speaking, there are two ways to develop faith in the Three Jewels. One is through learning about the qualities of the Buddha and the life he led, the other is through testing the Buddha's teachings in one's own experience and understanding.

—B. Alan Wallace, *Tibetan Buddhism from the Ground Up*

The great Indian teacher Nisargadatta Maharaj once said, "Wisdom tells me I am nothing. Love tells me I am everything. Between the two my life flows." "I am nothing" does not mean that there is a bleak wasteland within. It does mean that with awareness we open to a clear, unimpeded space, without center or periphery—nothing separate. If we are nothing, there is nothing at all to serve as a barrier to our boundless expression of love. Being nothing in this way, we are also, inevitably, everything. "Everything" does not mean self-aggrandizement, but a decisive recognition of interconnection; we are not separate. Both the clear, open space of "nothing" and the interconnectedness of "everything" awaken us to our true nature.

This is the truth we contact when we meditate, a sense of unity beyond suffering. It is always present; we merely need to be able to access it.

—Sharon Salzberg, *Lovingkindness*

The Buddhist challenge to conventional Western notions of spirituality illuminates the way we set flesh and spirit at war with each other. In Buddhism there is no original sin. Although noticing how we express our sexuality can certainly lead to an awareness of right conduct, the flesh is not regarded as representing a corruption or punishment of any kind, nor as an obstacle to the attainment of enlightenment. The root of human suffering is not sin, but our confusion about ego. We suffer because we believe in the existence of an individual self. This belief splits the world into "I" and "other."

—Stephen Butterfield, *Tricycle: The Buddhist Review,* Vol. I, #4

We are not innocent children victimized by a big bad world; if our world is big and bad, we made it that way. This is what the Buddha taught. The "other" is the child's boogeyman, the projection of our own fears onto a terrifying object of our imagination, which in turn terrorizes us. Our ignorance is not seeing that we are the other. We cannot afford to confuse innocence with this ignorance. Violence is not a permanent, immutable, fixed object. It is a state of mind, an expression of ignorance, with no more solid substance than a cloud. We cannot make a frontal attack on violence. Even protecting ourselves from it fuels its boogeyman existence. But the Buddha taught that we can change. This was his good news: that there is a way to alleviate suffering by freeing our minds from greed, anger, and ignorance. Yet until we apprehend the ways in which we are Oklahoma City, the bombs and the baby bears, the victims and the violators, we will continue to blame "them," all the while proclaiming our innocence and evading our responsibilities.

—Helen Tworkov, *Tricycle: The Buddhist Review,* Vol. V, #1

There is really no reason to kill our ordinary enemies; death will come to them naturally in the future anyway. Despite this fact there are some soldiers who engage in fearsome battles, willing to fight even though their enemies have superior weapons. They ignore the pains of battle and continue to fight until they are victorious. If there are people who are willing to expend such great effort in order to kill an ordinary enemy then why do we not strive unceasingly to destroy the worst enemy of all: the delusion that is the cause of all of our suffering? To overcome such a powerful foe we must certainly expect to experience great hardships but is there any need to mention the absolute necessity of attacking this enemy diligently?

—Geshe Kelsang Gyatso, *Meaningful to Behold*

Metta is to be extended towards all beings and all manifestations, yet most of our difficulties lie with people. It is much easier to love birds, dogs, cats and trees than it is to love people. Trees and animals don't answer back, but people do, so this is where our training commences. . . . Sometimes people find they don't feel anything while practicing metta meditation. That is nothing to worry about; thoughts aimed often enough in the right direction eventually produce the feelings. All our sense contacts produce feelings. Thoughts are the sixth sense, and even if we are only thinking metta, eventually the feeling will arise. It is one means of helping us to gain this heart quality, but certainly not the only one.

In our daily activities all of us are confronted with other people and often with those whom we would rather avoid. These are our challenges, lessons and tests. If we consider them in that manner we won't be so irritated by these experiences. . . . When we realize that such a confrontation is exactly what we need at that moment in order to overcome resistance and negativity and substitute *metta* for those emotions, then we will be grateful for the opportunity.

—Ayya Khema, *When the Iron Eagle Flies*

I have spent many hours catching insects in a cup and taking them outside. We can do that. We can change our relationship to other living creatures. This is not to suggest that the answers are always clear-cut and easy. If termites are eating up your house, what do you do? Do you say, "Be happy, be happy"? Or do you call the exterminator? Ethical decisions are not always easy. But we can become committed to training ourselves to look for alternatives to killing. We can practice not killing, and can take that practice further than we have.

—Joseph Goldstein, *Transforming the Mind, Healing the World*

The basic precepts are not passive. They can actively express a compassionate heart in our life. Not killing can grow into a reverence for life, a protective caring for all sentient beings who share life with us. Not stealing can become the basis for a wise ecology, honoring the limited resources of the earth and actively seeking ways to live and work that share our blessings worldwide. From this spirit can come a life of natural and healing simplicity. Out of not lying we can develop our voice to speak for compassion, understanding, and justice. Out of nonharming sexuality, our most intimate relations can also become expressions of love, joy, and tenderness. Out of not abusing intoxicants or becoming heedless, we can develop a spirit that seeks to live in the most awake and conscious manner in all circumstances.

At first, precepts are a practice. Then they become a necessity, and finally they become a joy. When our heart is awakened, they spontaneously illuminate our way in the world.

—Jack Kornfield, *A Path with Heart*

Abandon evildoing;
Practice virtue well;
Subdue your mind:
This is the Buddha's teaching.

Like a star, an optical illusion, or a flame,
A magical illusion, a dewdrop, or a bubble,
Like a dream, a flash of lightning, or a cloud—
So should one consider all compounded things.

While reciting [Shantideva's] words, we should reflect on impermanence and the lack of reality in phenomena . . .

—The Dalai Lama, *A Flash of Lightning in the Dark of Night*

Lack of understanding of the true nature of happiness, it seems to me, is the principal reason why people inflict sufferings on others. They think either that the other's pain may somehow be a cause of happiness for themselves or that their own happiness is more important, regardless of what pain it may cause. But this is shortsighted, no one truly benefits from causing harm to another sentient being. Whatever immediate advantage is gained at the expense of someone else is shortlived. In the long run causing others misery and infringing their rights to peace and happiness result in anxiety, fear and suspicion within oneself. Such feelings undermine the peace of mind and contentment which are the marks of happiness.

True happiness comes not from a limited concern for one's own well-being, or that of those one feels close to, but from developing love and compassion for all sentient beings. Here, love means wishing that all sentient beings should find happiness, and compassion means wishing that they should all be free of suffering. The development of this attitude gives rise to a sense of openness and trust that provides the basis for peace.

—The Dalai Lama, *The Dalai Lama: A Policy of Kindness,*
edited by Sidney Piburn

See everybody as the Buddha. When you are stuck in a traffic jam on the Los Angeles freeway, can you look at all the other drivers, particularly the ones who are weaving in and out of lanes, and see them as the Buddha? In a work situation, if you have a particularly cantankerous boss who you think is a complete idiot, can you look at that person as the Buddha? As a manager, can you see the person who is working for you as the Buddha?

—Gerry Shishin Wick Sensei, *Tricycle: The Buddhist Review,* Vol. V, #4

Those who seek liberation for themselves alone cannot become fully enlightened. Though it may be said that one who is not already liberated cannot liberate others, the very process of forgetting oneself to help others is itself liberating.

Therefore those who seek to benefit themselves alone actually harm themselves by doing so, while those who help others also help themselves by doing so.

—Muso Kokushi, *Dream Conversations*

I like that the point of convergence of liberation theology, Islamic mysticism, and engaged Buddhism is the sense of love that leads to commitment and involvement with the world, and not a turning away from the world. A form of wisdom that I strive for is the ability to know what is needed at a given moment in time. When do I need to reside in that location of stillness and contemplation, and when do I need to get up off my ass and do whatever is needed to be done in terms of physical work, or engagement with others, or confrontation with others? I'm not interested in ranking one type of action over the other.

—bell hooks, *Tricycle: The Buddhist Review*, Vol. II, #1

I gave up my house
and set out into homelessness.
I gave up my child, my cattle,
and all that I loved.
I gave up desire and hate.
My ignorance was thrown out.
I pulled out craving
along with its root.
Now I am quenched and still.

—Sangha, in Susan Murcott's *The First Buddhist Women*

With persistent practice, consciousness may eventually be perceived or felt as an entity of mere luminosity and knowing, to which anything is capable of appearing and which, when appropriate conditions arise, can be generated in the image of whatsoever object. As long as the mind does not encounter the external circumstance of conceptuality, it will abide empty without anything appearing in it, like clear water. Its very entity is that of mere experience. Let the mind flow of its own accord without conceptual overlay. Let the mind rest in its natural state, and observe it. In the beginning, when you are not used to this practice, it is quite difficult, but in time the mind appears like clear water.

—The Dalai Lama, *The Dalai Lama: A Policy of Kindness,*
edited by Sidney Piburn

"There is, monks, this one way to the purification of beings, for the overcoming of sorrow and distress, for the disappearance of pain and sadness, for the gaining of the right path, for the realization of Nibbana:—that is to say the four foundations of mindfulness.

"What are the four? Here, monks, a monk abides contemplating body as body, ardent, clearly aware and mindful, having put aside hankering and fretting for the world; he abides contemplating feelings as feelings . . . he abides contemplating mind as mind . . . he abides contemplating mind-objects as mind-objects, ardent, clearly aware and mindful, having put aside hankering and fretting for the world."

—Mahasatipatthana Sutta: The Greater Discourse on the
Foundations of Mindfulness, in *Thus Have I Heard:*
The Long Discourses of the Buddha,
trans. by Maurice Walshe

2. "And how, monks, does a monk abide contemplating the body as body? Here a monk, having gone into the forest, or to the root of a tree, or to an empty place, sits down crosslegged, holding his body erect, having established mindfulness before him. Mindfully he breathes in, mindfully he breathes out. Breathing in a long breath, he knows that he breathes in a long breath, and breathing out a long breath, he knows that he breathes out a long breath. Breathing in a short breath, he knows that he breathes in a short breath, and breathing out a short breath, he knows that he breathes out a short breath. He trains himself, thinking: 'I will breathe in, conscious of the whole body.' He trains himself, thinking: 'I will breathe out, conscious of the whole body.' He trains himself, thinking: 'I will breathe in, calming the whole bodily process.' He trains himself, thinking: 'I will breathe out, calming the whole bodily process.' . . . And he abides independent, not clinging to anything in the world. And that, monks, is how a monk abides contemplating body as body."

—Mahasatipatthana Sutta: The Greater Discourse on the
Foundations of Mindfulness, in *Thus Have I Heard:
The Long Discourses of the Buddha,*
trans. by Maurice Walshe

11. "And how, monks, does a monk abide contemplating feelings as feelings? Here, a monk feeling a pleasant feeling knows that he feels a pleasant feeling; feeling a painful feeling he knows that he feels a painful feeling; feeling a feeling that is neither-painful-nor-pleasant he knows that he feels a feeling that is neither-painful-nor-pleasant; feeling a pleasant sensual feeling he knows that he feels a pleasant sensual feeling; feeling a pleasant non-sensual feeling he knows that he feels a pleasant non-sensual feeling; feeling a painful sensual feeling . . . feeling a painful non-sensual feeling . . . feeling a sensual feeling that is neither-painful-nor-pleasant . . . feeling a non-sensual feeling that is neither-painful-nor-pleasant, he knows that he feels a non-sensual feeling that is neither-painful-nor-pleasant. . . . And he abides independent, not clinging to anything in the world. And that, monks, is how a monk abides contemplating feelings as feelings."

—Mahasatipatthana Sutta: The Greater Discourse on the
Foundations of Mindfulness, in *Thus Have I Heard:
The Long Discourses of the Buddha,*
trans. by Maurice Walshe

12. "And how, monks, does a monk abide contemplating mind as mind? Here, a monk knows a lustful mind as lustful, a mind free from lust as free from lust; a hating mind as hating, a mind free from hate as free from hate; a deluded mind as deluded, an undeluded mind as undeluded; a contracted mind as contracted, a distracted mind as distracted; a developed mind as developed, an undeveloped mind as undeveloped; a surpassed mind as surpassed, an unsurpassed mind as unsurpassed; a concentrated mind as concentrated, an unconcentrated mind as unconcentrated; a liberated mind as liberated, an unliberated mind as unliberated. . . . And he abides detached, not grasping at anything in the world. And that, monks, is how a monk abides contemplating mind as mind."

—Mahasatipatthana Sutta: The Greater Discourse on the
Foundations of Mindfulness, in *Thus Have I Heard:
The Long Discourses of the Buddha,*
trans. by Maurice Walshe

17. "Again, monks, a monk abides contemplating mind-objects as mind-objects in respect of the Four Noble Truths. How does he do so? Here, a monk knows as it really is: 'This is suffering'; he knows as it really is: 'This is the origin of suffering'; he knows as it really is: 'This is the cessation of suffering'; he knows as it really is: 'This is the way of practice leading to the cessation of suffering.'

18. "And what, monks, is the Noble Truth of Suffering? Birth is suffering, aging is suffering, death is suffering, sorrow, lamentation, pain, sadness and distress are suffering. Being attached to the unloved is suffering, being separated from the loved is suffering, not getting what one wants is suffering. In short, the five aggregates of grasping . . . are suffering."

—Mahasatipatthana Sutta: The Greater Discourse on the
Foundations of Mindfulness, in *Thus Have I Heard:
The Long Discourses of the Buddha,*
trans. by Maurice Walshe

What does it mean to be mindful? It means to be fully aware right here, concentrating on what is going on inside. . . . But mindfulness is not necessarily concentrating on an object. Being aware of confusion is also being mindful. If we have all kinds of things coming at our senses—noises, people demanding this and that—we cannot concentrate on any one of them for very long. But we can be aware of the confusion, or the excitement, or the impingement; we can be aware of the reactions in our own minds. That is what we call being mindful.

—Ajahn Sumedho, *Teachings of a Buddhist Monk*

When I was four years old, my mother used to bring me a cookie every time she came home from the market. I always went to the front yard and took my time eating it, sometimes half an hour or forty-five minutes for one cookie. I would take a small bite and look up at the sky. Then I would touch the dog with my feet and take another small bite. I just enjoyed being there, with the sky, the earth, the bamboo thickets, the cat, the dog, the flowers. I was able to do that because I did not have much to worry about. I did not think of the future, I did not regret the past. I was entirely in the present moment, with my cookie, the dog, the bamboo thickets, the cat, and everything.

It is possible to eat our meals as slowly and joyfully as I ate the cookie of my childhood. Maybe you have the impression that you have lost the cookie of your childhood, but I am sure it is still there, somewhere in your heart. Everything is still there, and if you really want it, you can find it. Eating mindfully is a most important practice of meditation.

—Thich Nhat Hanh, *Peace Is Every Step*

Speech is a powerful force. But how much attention do we pay to our speech? . . . Do we actually bring some wisdom and sensitivity to our speaking? What is behind our speech, what motivates it? Does something really have to be said?

When I was first getting into the practice of thinking and learning about speech, I conducted an experiment. For several months I decided not to speak about any third person; I would not speak to somebody about somebody else. No gossip. Ninety percent of my speech was eliminated. Before I did that, I had no idea that I had spent so much time and energy engaged in that kind of talking. It is not that my speech had been particularly malicious, but for the most part it had been useless. I found it tremendously interesting to watch the impact this experiment had on my mind. As I stopped speaking in this way, I found that one way or another a lot of my speech had been a judgment about somebody else. By stopping such speech for a while, my mind became less judgmental, not only of others, but also of myself, and it was a great relief.

—Joseph Goldstein, *Transforming the Mind, Healing the World*

Entry-level Right Speech is speech that doesn't add pain to any situation. This takes care of the obvious mistakes, like telling lies or purposely using speech hurtfully. High-level Right Speech maintains the balance of situations by not adding the destabilizing element of gossip.

Gossiping is talking about someone not present. Except on rare occasions when one might need to convey a need on behalf of another person, gossip is extra. Talking disparagingly about a third person is inviting the listener to share your grumbly mind space. Talking admiringly about a third person might cause your listener to feel unimportant. Why not choose to talk about current experience?

—Sylvia Boorstein, *It's Easier Than You Think*

Right speech means abstention (1) from telling lies, (2) from backbiting and slander and talk that may bring about hatred, enmity, disunity and disharmony among individuals or groups of people, (3) from harsh, rude, impolite, malicious and abusive language, and (4) from idle, useless and foolish babble and gossip. When one abstains from these forms of wrong and harmful speech one naturally has to speak the truth, has to use words that are friendly and benevolent, pleasant and gentle, meaningful and useful. One should not speak carelessly: speech should be at the right time and place. If one cannot say something useful, one should keep "noble silence."

—Walpola Rahula, *What the Buddha Taught*

Morality as taught by way of rules is extremely powerful and valuable in the development of practice. It must be remembered first that it, like all the techniques in meditation, is merely a tool to enable one to eventually get to that place of unselfishness where morality and wisdom flow naturally. In the West, there's a myth that freedom means free expression—that to follow all desires wherever they take one is true freedom. In fact, as one observes the mind, one sees that following desires, attractions, repulsions is not at all freedom, but is a kind of bondage. A mind filled with desires and grasping inevitably entails great suffering. Freedom is not to be gained through the ability to perform certain external actions. True freedom is an inward state of being. Once it is attained, no situation in the world can bind one or limit one's freedom. It is in this context that we must understand moral precepts and moral rules.

—Jack Kornfield, *Living Dharma*

"Discipline" is a difficult word for most of us. It conjures up images of somebody standing over you with a stick, telling you that you're wrong. But self-discipline is different. It's the skill of seeing through the hollow shouting of your own impulses and piercing their secret. They have no power over you. It's all a show, a deception. Your urges scream and bluster at you; they cajole; they coax; they threaten; but they really carry no stick at all. You give in out of habit. You give in because you never really bother to look beyond the threat. It is all empty back there. There is only one way to learn this lesson, though. The words on this page won't do it. But look within and watch the stuff coming up—restlessness, anxiety, impatience, pain—just watch it come up and don't get involved. Much to your surprise, it will simply go away. It rises, it passes away. As simple as that. There is another word for self-discipline. It is patience.

—Henepola Gunaratana, *Mindfulness in Plain English*

We can never obtain peace in the world if we neglect the inner world and don't make peace with ourselves. World peace must develop out of inner peace. Without inner peace it is impossible to achieve world peace, external peace. Weapons themselves do not act. They have not come out of the blue. Man has made them. But even given those weapons, those terrible weapons, they cannot act by themselves. As long as they are left alone in storage they cannot do any harm. A human being must use them. Someone must push the button. Satan, the evil powers, cannot push that button. Human beings must do it.

—The Dalai Lama, *The Dalai Lama: A Policy of Kindness,*
edited by Sidney Piburn

If we had to make a choice between outer pleasure, comfort and peace, and inner freedom and ultimate happiness, we should choose inner peace. If we could find that within, then the outer would take care of itself. Even when we have a comfortable and pleasant life externally, if our inner peace is shattered, or disturbed, we are not able to enjoy all that we have in our outer life. To make that transformation we find—when we think only of ourselves, and hold on to things, consider ourselves and our happiness as the most important thing—that it is the ego and its clinging that disturbs both the outer and the inner happiness. Even if we have a well-organized outer life, it can be very difficult for us to find inner happiness because we can never be satisfied so long as we have not cut the attachments due to ego. There is no end to it—it wants more and more—without any limit. The ego is insatiable.

—Dilgo Khyentse Rinpoche,
Tricycle: The Buddhist Review, Vol. I, #3

It is a great turning point in our spiritual lives when we go from an intellectual appreciation of a path to the heartfelt confidence that says, "Yes, it is possible to awaken. I can, too." A tremendous joy accompanies this confidence. When we place our hearts upon the practice, the teachings come alive. That turning point, which transforms an abstract concept of a spiritual path into our own personal path, is faith.

—Sharon Salzberg, *Tricycle: The Buddhist Review,* Vol. VI, #3

You might think that if you let go of your ego world, you might become passive and defenseless like some kind of crash dummy, and people will take advantage of you. Or that you might wander around aimlessly in the street without an agenda. If this were the case, as one contemporary Buddhist master pointed out, it would be necessary to have enlightenment wards in hospitals to take care of bruised or socially inoperative buddhas. But this is not the case. Rather than being inmate types, people who have become enlightened to any degree are builders of hospitals for other people. Their intelligence and compassion are relatively unobstructed, and they tend to become quite active and effective citizens.

—Samuel Bercholz, *Entering the Stream*

180. Having accumulated suffering for no purpose
Because of my honoring and serving this body,
What use is attachment and anger
For this thing that is similar to a piece of wood?

181. Whether I am caring for my body in this way,
Or whether it is being eaten by vultures,
It has no attachment or hatred towards these things—
Why then am I so attached to it?

182. If (my body) knows no anger when derided
And no pleasure when praised,
For what reason
Am I wearing myself out like this?

—Shantideva, *A Guide to the Bodhisattva's Way of Life,*
trans. by Stephen Batchelor

I always say that there's a kind of implicit mindfulness and wisdom in metta practice. The very process of letting go of a distraction implies in some way seeing its transparency, not freaking out over it, not being angry about it, not getting involved with it, not identifying with it. You may not consciously say to yourself, "Oh, look, this moment is changing," but you can't let go of the distraction unless you are actually seeing that. You would be trying to push it away from anger rather than actually letting go. So to do the metta practice, you actually bring forth that level of wisdom.

—Sharon Salzberg, *Spirit Rock Meditation Center Newsletter,* 1997

[W]hen we realize that we are forced to change positions because of pain, we should question further to find out if there are other reasons. If the answer is that we change because we want to be comfortable, this is incorrect. It is incorrect because it is a distortion of happiness. The correct answer is that we change in order to "cure" the pain. We do not change to acquire happiness. The wrong answer comes from misunderstanding, and if we do not have the right comprehension when we change positions, defilements can and will spring up.

Changing positions to "cure" pain indicates that we have to remedy the situation at all times. We should not misjudge and think that the reason is to attain happiness, since the curing of pain all the time is the same as having to take medicines constantly. It is like nursing a continuous sickness. Thus, we should not look upon nursing sickness and curing pain as being happiness at all.

—Achaan Naeb, in Jack Kornfield's *Living Dharma*

It is hardest to cure a disease when the medicine we take itself *causes* the disease. We scratch the itch, and the scratching only makes it worse, we try to quench our thirst by drinking salt water, and we make ourselves thirstier. This is what happens when we believe that the only way to end desires is to fulfill them.

A different and liberating insight dawns when we begin to pay careful attention to this powerful energy in our lives.

—Joseph Goldstein, *Insight Meditation*

Our minds are used to thinking, but when we want to become calm and peaceful that is exactly what we have to stop doing. It is easier said than done, because the mind will continue to do what it is used to doing. There is another reason why it finds it difficult to refrain from its habits: thinking is the only ego support we have while we are meditating, and particularly when we keep noble silence. "I think, therefore I am." Western philosophy accepts that as an absolute. Actually it is a relative truth, which all of us experience.

When we are thinking, we know that we are here; when there is no chattering in the mind, we believe we lose control. . . . Our first difficulty is that although we would like to become peaceful and calm and have no thoughts, our mind does not want to obey. . . . So instead of trying over and over again to become calm we can use whatever arises to gain some insight. A little bit of insight brings a little bit of calm, and a little bit of calm brings a little bit of insight.

—Ayya Khema, *When the Iron Eagle Flies*

The purpose of meditation is not to concentrate on the breath, without interruption, forever. That by itself would be a useless goal. The purpose of meditation is not to achieve a perfectly still and serene mind. Although a lovely state, it doesn't lead to liberation by itself. The purpose of meditation is to achieve uninterrupted mindfulness. Mindfulness, and only mindfulness, produces Enlightenment.

Distractions come in all sizes, shapes and flavors. Buddhist philosophy has organized them into categories. One of them is the category of hindrances. They are called hindrances because they block your development of both components of meditation, mindfulness and concentration. A bit of caution on this term: The word "hindrances" carries a negative connotation, and indeed these are states of mind we want to eradicate. That does not mean, however, that they are to be repressed, avoided, or condemned.

Let's use greed as an example. We wish to avoid prolonging any state of greed that arises, because a continuation of that state leads to bondage and sorrow. That does not mean we try to toss the thought out of the mind when it appears. We simply refuse to encourage it to stay. We let it come, and we let it go.

—Henepola Gunaratana, *Mindfulness in Plain English*

A . . . great distraction at times are so-called "running commentary" thoughts such as, "Now I am not thinking of anything," "Things are going very well now," "This is dreadful; my mind just won't stay still" and the like. . . . All such thoughts should simply be noted as "Thinking," and, as Huang Po says, just "dropped like a piece of rotten wood." "Dropped," notice, not *thrown* down. A piece of rotten wood is not doing anything to irritate you, but is just of no use, so there is no point in hanging on to it. . . . Nor is there any need to try to retrace the links in a chain of associated thoughts, nor to try to ascertain what it was that first started the chain. Any such impulse should itself be noted simply as "Thinking," and the mind should revert to the breathing. However badly things have just been going, one should take up again at the only place one can—where one is—and go on from there.

—Bhikkhu Mangalo, *The Practice of Recollection*

When perception is stronger than mindfulness, we recognize various appearances and create concepts such as "body," "car," "house," or "person" . . .

On some clear night, go outside, look up at the sky, and see if you can find the Big Dipper. For most people that is a familiar constellation, easy to pick out from all the other stars. But is there really a Big Dipper up there in the sky?

There is no Big Dipper up there. "Big Dipper" is a concept. Humans looked, saw a certain pattern, and then created a concept in our collective mind to describe it. That concept is useful because it helps us recognize the constellation. But it also has another, less useful effect. By creating the concept "Big Dipper," we separate out those stars from all the rest, and then, if we become attached to the idea of that separation, we lose the sense of the night sky's wholeness, its oneness. Does the separation actually exist in the sky? No. We created it through the use of a concept.

Does anything change in the sky when we understand that there is no Big Dipper? No.

—Joseph Goldstein, *Insight Meditation*

In a famous parable, the Buddha imagines a group of blind men who are invited to identify an elephant. One takes the tail and says it's a rope; another clasps a leg and says it's a pillar; another feels the side and says it's a wall; another holds the trunk and says it's a tube. Depending on which part of Buddhism you grasp, you might identify it as a system of ethics, a philosophy, a contemplative psychotherapy, a religion. While containing all of these, it can no more be reduced to any one of them than an elephant can be reduced to its tail.

—Stephen Batchelor, *Buddhism Without Beliefs*

Buddhism stands unique in the history of human thought in denying the existence of . . . a Soul, Self, or *Atman*. According to the teaching of the Buddha, the idea of self is an imaginary, false belief which has no corresponding reality, and it produces harmful thoughts of "me" and "mine," selfish desire, craving, attachment, hatred, ill-will, conceit, pride, egoism, and other defilements, impurities and problems. It is the source of all the troubles in the world from personal conflicts to wars between nations. In short, to this false view can be traced all the evil in the world.

—Walpola Rahula, *What the Buddha Taught*

Sitting astride the senses is a shadowy, phantomlike figure with insatiable desires and a lust for dominance. His name? Ego, Ego the Magician, and the deadly tricks he carries up his sleeve are delusive thinking, greed, and anger. Where he came from no one knows, but he has surely been around as long as the human mind. This wily and slippery conjurer deludes us into believing that we can only enjoy the delights of the senses without pain by delivering ourselves into his hands.

Of the many devices employed by Ego to keep us in his power, none is more effective than language. The English language is so structured that it demands the repeated use of the personal pronoun "I" for grammatical nicety and presumed clarity. . . . All this plays into the hands of Ego, strengthening our servitude and enlarging our sufferings, for the more we postulate this I the more we are exposed to Ego's never-ending demands.

—Philip Kapleau, in Thich Nhat Hanh's *Zen Keys*

Ordinarily, we spend all our time comparing and discriminating between this and that, always looking around for something good to happen to us. And because of that, we become restless and anxious about everything. As long as we are able to imagine something better than what we have or who we are, it follows naturally that there could also be something worse. We are constantly pursued by misgivings that something bad will happen. In other words, as long as we live by distinguishing between the better way and the worse way, we can never find absolute peace such that whatever happens is all right. This anxiety or lack of peace of mind is like that felt by the Japanese high-school student aiming to succeed in the entrance exams.

When we let go of our thoughts that distinguish better from worse and instead see everything in terms of the Universal Self, we are able to settle upon a different attitude toward life—the attitude of magnanimous mind that whatever happens, we are living out Self which is only Self. Here a truly peaceful life unfolds.

—Kosho Uchiyama, *Opening the Hand of Thought*

In the broadest conception of the path, in the vast context of spiritual practice, we cultivate and nourish certain qualities that support and propel us forward into freedom. The Pali word *parami* refers to ten wholesome qualities in our minds and the accumulated power they bring to us: generosity, morality, renunciation, wisdom, energy, patience, truthfulness, resolve, lovingkindness, and equanimity. . . . Parami does not come from some being outside ourselves; rather, it comes from our own gradually accumulated purity. A Buddhist understanding of reliance on a higher power would not necessarily involve reliance on some supernormal being. It is, rather, a reliance on these forces of purity in ourselves that are outside our small, constricted sense of I, and that constitute the source of grace in our lives.

—Joseph Goldstein, *Insight Meditation*

The view of interdependence makes for a great openness of mind. In general, instead of realizing that what we experience arises from a complicated network of causes, we tend to attribute happiness or sadness, for example, to single, individual sources. But if this were so, as soon as we came into contact with what we consider to be good, we would be automatically happy, and conversely, in the case of bad things, invariably sad. The causes of joy and sorrow would be easy to identify and target. It would all be very simple, and there would be good reason for our anger and attachment. When, on the other hand, we consider that everything we experience results from a complex interplay of causes and conditions, we find that there is no single thing to desire or resent, and it is more difficult for the afflictions of attachment or anger to arise. In this way, the view of interdependence makes our minds more relaxed and open.

—The Dalai Lama, *A Flash of Lightning in the Dark of Night*

Buddha told a parable in a sutra:

A man traveling across a field encountered a tiger. He fled, the tiger after him. Coming to a precipice, he caught hold of the root of a wild vine and swung himself down over the edge. The tiger sniffed at him from above. Trembling, the man looked down to where, far below, another tiger was waiting to eat him. Only the vine sustained him.

Two mice, one white and one black, little by little started to gnaw away the vine. The man saw a luscious strawberry near him. Grasping the vine with one hand, he plucked the strawberry with the other. How sweet it tasted!

—Paul Reps, *Zen Flesh, Zen Bones*

The enlightenment of the Buddha was not primarily a religious discovery. It was not a mystical encounter with "God" or a god. It was not the reception of a divine mission to spread the "Truth" of "God" in the world. The Buddha's enlightenment was rather a human being's direct, exact, and comprehensive experience of the final nature and total structure of reality. It was the culmination for all time of the manifest ideals of any tradition of philosophical exploration or scientific investigation. "Buddha" is not a personal name; it is a title, meaning "awakened," "enlightened," and "evolved." A Buddha's enlightenment is a *perfect omniscience*. A Buddha's mind is what theists have thought the mind of God would have to be like, totally knowing of every single detail of everything in an infinite universe, totally aware of everything—hence by definition inconceivable, incomprehensible to finite, ignorant, egocentric consciousness.

—Robert A. F. Thurman, *Essential Tibetan Buddhism*

We can demonstrate that the experience of steady practice influences the quality of our lives, but the nature of the essential urge toward enlightenment *is* enlightenment itself. The very fact that we are intrigued with the spiritual quest stems from the source of the Light, so to speak. Consequently, enlightenment is not an end; it is truer to say that it is the beginning.

—David A. Cooper, *Silence, Simplicity and Solitude*

A wonderful painting is the result of the feeling in your fingers. If you have the feeling of the thickness of the ink in your brush, the painting is already there before you paint. When you dip your brush into the ink you already know the result of your drawing, or else you cannot paint. So before you do something, "being" is there, the result is there. Even though you look as if you were sitting quietly, all your activity, past and present, is included; and the result of your sitting is also already there. You are not resting at all. All the activity is included within you. That is your being. So all results of your practice are included in your sitting. This is our practice, our zazen.

—Shunryu Suzuki, *Zen Mind, Beginner's Mind*

As Shantideva says, there are many beings to whom one can make charity, but there are very few beings with respect to whom one can practice patience, and what is more rare is more valuable. An enemy is really most kind. Through cultivating patience one's power of merit increases, and the practice of patience can only be done in dependence upon an enemy. For this reason, enemies are the main instigators of the increase of meritorious power. An enemy is not someone who prevents the practice of religion but someone who helps practice.

—The Dalai Lama, *The Meaning of Life from a Buddhist Perspective*

Bodhidharma brought Zen Buddhism from India to China. He was well known for being fierce and uncompromising. There is a story about how he kept nodding off during meditation, so he cut off his eyelids. When he threw them on the ground, they turned into a tea plant, and then he realized he could simply drink the tea to stay awake! He was uncompromising in that he wanted to know what was true, and he wasn't going to take anybody else's word for it. His big discovery was that by looking directly into our own heart, we find the awakened Buddha, the completely unclouded experience of how things really are.

—Pema Chödrön, *When Things Fall Apart:
Heart Advice for Difficult Times*

It is not merely enthusiasm that erodes when practice declines. Your body and mind go out of tune. You are no longer a vessel of insight. The cardinal can sing; the wind can move the iron-wood trees delicately; a child can ask a wise question—and where is your center? How can you respond?

It is time to put yourself back in tune, to be ready for experiences that make life fulfilling. Take up the advice for beginners. Put your zazen pad somewhere between your bathroom and your kitchen. Sit down there in the morning after you use the bathroom and before you cook breakfast. You are sitting with everyone in the world. If you can sit only briefly, you will have at least settled your day.

—Robert Aitken, *Encouraging Words*

The moment we want happiness, we start to cling to it in our mind. First, we cling to our own idea of happiness. We relate to the outside world as a source of satisfaction and look outward for the things we normally associate with happiness—accumulating wealth, success, fame or power. As soon as we become attached to any idea—happiness, success or whatever—there is already some stress. Clinging is itself a stressful state, and everything that derives from it is also stressful. For example, try to clench your hand to make a fist. As soon as you start to clench your hand, you have to use energy to keep your fingers clenched tightly. When you let go of the clenching, your hand is free again.

So it is with the mind. When it is in such a state of clenching, it can never be free. It can never experience peace or happiness, even if one has all the wealth, fame and power in the world.

—Thynn Thynn, *Living Meditation, Living Insight*

What happens when we do not let go? Asians have a very clever trap for catching monkeys. People hollow out a coconut, put something sweet in it, and make a hole in the bottom of the coconut just big enough for the monkey to slide its open hand in, but not big enough for the monkey to withdraw its hand as a fist. They attach the coconut to a tree, and the monkey comes along and gets trapped. What keeps the monkey trapped? Only the force of desire, of clinging, of attachment. All the monkey has to do is let go of the sweet, open its hand, slip it out, and be free. But only a very rare monkey will do that.

—Joseph Goldstein, *Transforming the Mind, Healing the World*

Becoming, which results from clinging, involves the idea of having or being something more satisfying than at present. We want to become a very good meditator, or we want to become spiritual, or more learned. We have all sorts of ideas but all are bound up with wanting to become, because we are not satisfied with what we are. Often we do not even pay attention to what we are now, but just know that something is lacking. Instead of trying to realize what we are and investigating where the difficulty actually lies, we just dream of becoming something else. When we have become something or someone else, we can be just as dissatisfied as before.

—Ayya Khema, *When the Iron Eagle Flies*

Let's try an experiment. Pick up a coin. Imagine that it represents the object at which you are grasping. Hold it tightly clutched in your fist and extend your arm, with the palm of your hand facing the ground. Now if you let go or relax your grip, you will lose what you are clinging onto. That's why you hold on.

But there's another possibility: You can let go and yet keep hold of it. With your arm still outstretched, turn your hand over so that it faces the sky. Release your hand and the coin still rests on your open palm. You let go. And the coin is still yours, even with all this space around it.

So there is a way in which we can accept impermanence and still relish life, at one and the same time, without grasping.

—Sogyal Rinpoche, *The Tibetan Book of Living and Dying*

The near enemies are qualities that arise in the mind and masquerade as genuine spiritual realization, when in fact they are only an imitation, serving to separate us from true feeling rather than connecting us to it. . . .

The near enemy of loving-kindness is attachment. . . . At first, attachment may feel like love, but as it grows it becomes more clearly the opposite, characterized by clinging, controlling, and fear.

The near enemy of compassion is pity, and this also separates us. Pity feels sorry for "that poor person over there," as if he were somehow different from us. . . .

The near enemy of sympathetic joy (the joy in the happiness of others) is comparison, which looks to see if we have more of, the same as, or less than another. . . .

The near enemy of equanimity is indifference. True equanimity is balance in the midst of experience, whereas indifference is a withdrawal and not caring, based on fear. . . .

If we do not recognize and understand the near enemies, they will deaden our spiritual practice. The compartments they make cannot shield us for long from the pain and unpredictability of life, but they will surely stifle the joy and open connectedness of true relationships.

—Jack Kornfield, *A Path with Heart*

Nonviolence belongs to a continuum from the personal to the global, and from the global to the personal. One of the most significant Buddhist interpretations of nonviolence concerns the application of this ideal to daily life. Nonviolence is not some exalted regimen that can be practiced only by a monk or a master; it also pertains to the way one interacts with a child, vacuums a carpet, or waits in line. Besides the more obvious forms of violence, whenever we separate ourselves from a given situation (for example, through inattentiveness, negative judgments, or impatience), we "kill" something valuable. However subtle it may be, such violence actually leaves victims in its wake: people, things, one's own composure, the moment itself. According to the Buddhist reckoning, these small-scale incidences of violence accumulate relentlessly, are multiplied on a social level, and become a source of the large-scale violence that can sweep down upon us so suddenly. . . . One need not wait until war is declared and bullets are flying to work for peace, Buddhism teaches. A more constant and equally urgent battle must be waged each day against the forces of one's own anger, carelessness, and self-absorption.

—Kenneth Kraft, *Inner Peace, World Peace*

The word [*karma*] penetrated the Western consciousness, from the Buddhist point of view at least, in somewhat distorted guise. It is often called the Law of Cause and Effect, so it is about the consequences of actions of body, speech and mind. And consequences are very important in Buddhism.

Any action that is willed, however subtly, by the person who performs it will always produce a future "ripening" and ultimately a "fruit" of similar moral quality, because in the human sphere karma operates in an ethical manner. So an unethical action will induce a come-back of like kind in this life or some future rebirth; and the same goes for morally good or indifferent actions that are willed and freely undertaken. In the Bible it says something similar: that we reap what we sow. If we want to progress spiritually—or even just to live with minimum aggravation—it therefore behooves us to be very careful how we speak and act, for there is no way we can escape the consequences.

—John Snelling, *Elements of Buddhism*

In a well-known phrase, the Buddha said, "Hatred can never cease by hatred. Hatred can only cease by love. This is an eternal law." We can begin to transcend the cycle of aversion when we can stop seeing ourselves personally as agents of revenge. Ultimately, all beings are the owners of their own karma. If someone has caused harm, they will suffer. If we have caused harm, we will suffer. As the Buddha said in the *Dhammapada*:

> We are what we think.
> All that we are arises with our thoughts.
> With our thoughts we make the world.
> Speak or act with an impure mind
> And trouble will follow you
> As the wheel follows the ox that draws the cart. . . .
> Speak or act with a pure mind
> And happiness will follow you
> As your shadow, unshakable.

Happiness and unhappiness depend upon our actions.

—Sharon Salzberg, *Lovingkindness*

The meditative experience is, to my mind, the practice of dying, the practice of letting go. The more you practice letting go, the more you begin to understand the journey of your soul or your spirit as it detaches from the material nature of existence. There is a river, and as soon as you unmoor the boat and you start to enter that river, you end up on a journey. Not all of us have gone to the mouth of that river, but I think that we are all aware, in the meditative process, that the journey exists. As you go deeply inside your psyche you're aware of the similarity of *this* journey to the journey of the soul after death.

—Bruce Rubin, *Tricycle: The Buddhist Review,* Vol. I, #1

If you look deeply into the palm of your hand, you will see your parents and all generations of your ancestors. All of them are alive in this moment. Each is present in your body. You are the continuation of each of these people.

To be born means that something which did not exist comes into existence. But the day we are "born" is not our beginning. It is a day of continuation. But that should not make us less happy when we celebrate our "Happy Continuation Day."

Since we are never born, how can we cease to be? This is what the *Heart Sutra* reveals to us. When we have a tangible experience of non-birth and non-death, we know ourselves beyond duality. The meditation on "no separate self" is one way to pass through the gate of birth and death.

Your hand proves that you have never been born and you will never die. The thread of life has never been interrupted from time without beginning until now. Previous generations, all the way back to single-celled beings, are present in your hand at this moment. You can observe and experience this. Your hand is always available as a subject for meditation.

—Thich Nhat Hanh, *Present Moment, Wonderful Moment*

One of the most difficult things to learn is that mindfulness is not dependent on any emotional or mental state. We have certain images of meditation. Meditation is something done in quiet caves by tranquil people who move slowly. Those are training conditions. They are set up to foster concentration and to learn the skill of mindfulness. Once you have learned that skill, however, you can dispense with the training restrictions, and you should. You don't need to move at a snail's pace to be mindful. You don't even need to be calm. You can be mindful while solving problems in intensive calculus. You can be mindful in the middle of a football scrimmage. You can even be mindful in the midst of a raging fury. Mental and physical activities are no bar to mindfulness. If you find your mind extremely active, then simply observe the nature and degree of that activity. It is just a part of the passing show within.

—Henepola Gunaratana, *Mindfulness in Plain English*

You might try looking at all the stuff that comes up in your head as just a secretion. All our thoughts and feelings are a kind of secretion. It is important for us to see that clearly. I've always got things coming up in my head, but if I tried to act on everything that came up, it would just wear me out. Haven't you ever had the experience of being up on a very high place and having an urge to jump? That urge to jump is just a secretion in your head. If you felt that you had to follow every urge that came into your head, well . . .

—Kosho Uchiyama, *Opening the Hand of Thought*

110. Better than a hundred years lived in vice, without contemplation, is one single day of life lived in virtue and in deep concentration.

111. Better than a hundred years lived in ignorance, without contemplation, is one single day of life lived in wisdom and in deep concentration.

112. Better than a hundred years lived in idleness and in weakness is one single day of life lived with courage and powerful striving.

113. Better than a hundred years not considering how all things arise and pass away is one single day of life if one considers how all things arise and pass away.

114. Better than a hundred years not seeing one's own immortality is one single day if one sees one's own immortality.

115. Better than a hundred years not seeing the Path supreme is one single day of life if one sees the Path supreme.

—*The Dhammapada,* trans. by Juan Mascaro

According to the wisdom of Buddha, we *can* actually use our lives to prepare for death. We do not have to wait for the painful death of someone close to us or the shock of terminal illness to force us into looking at our lives. Nor are we condemned to go out empty-handed at death to meet the unknown. We can begin, here and now, to find meaning in our lives. We can make of every moment an opportunity to change and to prepare—wholeheartedly, precisely, and with peace of mind—for death and eternity.

In the Buddhist approach, life and death are seen as one whole, where death is the beginning of another chapter of life. Death is a mirror in which the entire meaning of life is reflected.

—Sogyal Rinpoche, *The Tibetan Book of Living and Dying*

Due to having made karma, rebirth consciousness arises. But we need not think of rebirth only in a future life. We are in actual fact reborn every moment with new thoughts and feelings, and we bring with us the karma that we made in past moments. If we were angry a moment ago, we are not going to feel good immediately. If we were loving a moment ago, we would be feeling fine now. Thus we live from moment to moment with the results of our *karma*.

Every morning, particularly, can be seen as a rebirth. The day is young, we are full of energy and have a whole day ahead of us. Every moment we get older and are tired enough in the evening to fall asleep and die a small death. All we can do then is toss and turn in bed, and our mind is dreamy and foggy. Every day can be regarded as a whole lifespan, since we can only live one day at a time; the past is gone and the future may or may not come; only this rebirth, this day, this moment, is important.

—Ayya Khema, *When the Iron Eagle Flies*

How is it that harmful results follow from harmful actions? It is by the force of an imprint placed on our mind that the potential to experience future suffering comes about. For example, a person who commits murder plants a very strong negative impression on his or her own mind and that impression, or seed, carries with it the potential to place that mind in a state of extreme misery. Unless the impression of that non-virtuous action is purified this latent seed will remain implanted in the mind, its power dormant but unimpaired. When the appropriate circumstances are eventually met, the potential power of this impression will be activated and the seed will ripen as an experience of intense suffering. . . .

The situation is analogous to that of an arid piece of ground into which seeds were placed a long time ago. As long as these seeds are not destroyed somehow, they will retain their potential to grow. Should the ground be watered sufficiently these long-forgotten seeds will suddenly sprout forth. In a similar fashion our karmic actions plant their seeds in the field of our consciousness and when we encounter the proper conditions these seeds will sprout and bear their karmic fruit.

—Geshe Kelsang Gyatso, *Meaningful to Behold*

Right livelihood has ceased to be a purely personal matter. It is our collective karma. Suppose I am a schoolteacher and I believe that nurturing love and understanding in children is a beautiful occupation. I would object if someone were to ask me to stop teaching and become, for example, a butcher. But when I meditate on the interrelatedness of all things, I can see that the butcher is not the only person responsible for killing animals. He does his work for all of us who eat meat. We are co-responsible for his act of killing. We may think the butcher's livelihood is wrong and ours is right, but if we didn't eat meat, he wouldn't have to kill, or he would kill less. Right livelihood is a collective matter. The livelihood of each person affects us all, and vice versa. The butcher's children may benefit from my teaching, while my children, because they eat meat, share some responsibility for the butcher's livelihood.

—Thich Nhat Hanh, in Claude Whitmyer's
Mindfulness and Meaningful Work

The Buddha gave five reasons why a moral person should desire to be possessed of means. Firstly, by his work, diligence and clear-sightedness he could make happy himself, his parents, wife and children, servants and workpeople. Secondly, he could make happy his friends and companions. Thirdly, he would be able to keep his property from the depredations of fire, water, rulers, robbers, enemies and heirs. Fourthly, he would be able to make suitable offerings to his kin, guests, deceased, kings, and devas. Fifthly, he would be able to institute, over a period, offerings to recluses and others who abstain from pride and negligence, who are established in patience and gentleness, and who are engaged in every way in perfecting themselves. At the same time, whether his wealth increases or whether it does not, he should not be disturbed in his mind if he knows that his reasons for trying to amass it were good.

—Hammalawa Saddhatissa, *Buddhist Ethics*

The most important step in building support for right liveli-hood is giving back more than you get. It's not really a matter of keeping track in some kind of ledger book. It's more a func-tion of the attitude that you adopt in caring for yourself and those around you. People tend to mirror the way that they are treated. If you show an interest in helping and sharing, those around you will start helping you and sharing more with you. If you empathize with other people's situations, they tend to empathize more with yours. . . . The key is to be active about it. Look for opportunities to cooperate. With a proactive atti-tude of supporting others, you will seldom experience a short-age of support from others.

A simple caution is in order, however, when it comes to giv-ing to others. . . . Give more than you get, but not more than you've got.

—Claude Whitmyer, *Mindfulness and Meaningful Work*

It is essential that our understanding be translated into practice, not with an idealistic vision that we suddenly will become totally loving and compassionate, but with a willingness to be just who we are and to start from there. Then our practice is grounded in the reality of our experience, rather than based on some expectation of how we should be. But we must begin. We work with the precepts as guidelines for harmonizing our actions in the world; we live with contentment and simplicity that does not exploit other people or the planet; we work with restraint in the mind, seeing that it's possible to say no to certain conditioned impulses, or to expand when we feel bound by inhibitions and fear; we reflect upon karma and the direction of our lives, where it is leading and what is being developed; we cultivate generosity and love, compassion and service. All of this together becomes our path of practice.

—Joseph Goldstein, *Seeking the Heart of Wisdom*

The goal of vipassana practice is to cultivate the mindful, non-reactive observation of bodily and mental processes so as to develop an increasing thorough awareness—an awareness undistorted by our usual desires, fears and views of the true nature of these processes, that they are impermanent, that they are without self and therefore involving suffering on our part until we learn to let go.

It is through mindful observation of what is actually there that the delusion that makes us perceive what is impermanent and transient as permanent and lasting is gradually dispelled. *Liberation consists in experiencing and understanding fully and clearly that everything is impermanent and seeing that there is quite literally nothing to worry about.*

—Amadeus Solé-Leris, *Tranquillity & Insight*

A fish swims in the ocean, and no matter how far it swims there is no end to the water. A bird flies in the sky, and no matter how far it flies there is no end to the air. However, the fish and the bird have never left their elements. When their activity is large their field is large. When their need is small their field is small. Thus, each of them totally covers its full range, and each of them totally experiences its realm. . . . Practice, enlightenment, and people are like this.

—Zen Master Dogen, *Moon in a Dewdrop,*
edited by Kazuaki Tanahashi

Buddhism is neither pessimistic nor optimistic. If anything at all, it is realistic, for it takes a realistic view of life and of the world. It looks at things objectively. It does not falsely lull you into living in a fool's paradise, nor does it frighten and agonize you with all kinds of imaginary fears and sins. It tells you exactly and objectively what you are and what the world around you is, and shows you the way to perfect freedom, peace, tranquillity and happiness.

One physician may gravely exaggerate an illness and give up hope altogether. Another may ignorantly declare that there is no illness and that no treatment is necessary, thus deceiving the patient with a false consolation. You may call the first one pessimistic and the second optimistic. Both are equally dangerous. But a third physician diagnoses the symptoms correctly, understands the cause and the nature of the illness, sees clearly that it can be cured and courageously administers a course of treatment, thus saving his patient. The Buddha is like the last physician. He is the wise and scientific doctor for the ills of the world.

—Walpola Rahula, *What the Buddha Taught*

At the time of the Buddha there was a monk who was so infatuated with the Buddha that he followed him around like a puppy dog. Wherever the Buddha went, this monk went too. One day the monk became very ill and had to stay in bed. As he was lying in bed he started crying. When the other monks came to see him . . . he said, "I am crying because, being ill, I can't see the Buddha."

Upon learning this, the Buddha immediately came to visit the sick monk, who brightened up and looked happy again. Then the Buddha said to him, "Whoever sees me, sees the *dhamma*; whoever sees the *dhamma*, sees me."

Whoever sees a Buddha, sees nothing but enlightenment, which is the essence of the *dhamma*. Whoever can see the *dhamma* within, sees the Buddha, equaling enlightenment. The greatest jewel is recognizing the *dhamma* in oneself and not being attached to any one person, even the Buddha, who only wants to be our guide. When true confidence arises in the *dhamma*, it gives great impetus to the practice.

—Ayya Khema, *When the Iron Eagle Flies*

Even before we practice it, enlightenment is there. But usually we understand the practice of zazen and enlightenment as two different things: here is practice, like a pair of glasses, and when we use the practice, like putting the glasses on, we see enlightenment. This is the wrong understanding. The glasses themselves are enlightenment, and to put them on is also enlightenment. So whatever you do, or even though you do not do anything, enlightenment is there, always. This is Bodhidharma's understanding of enlightenment.

—Shunryu Suzuki, *Zen Mind, Beginner's Mind*

Trying to find a Buddha or enlightenment is like trying to grab space. Space has a name but no form. It's not something you can pick up or put down. And you certainly can't grab it. Beyond this mind you'll never see a Buddha. The Buddha is a product of your mind. Why look for a Buddha beyond this mind?

—*The Zen Teachings of Bodhidharma*

How to make our lives an embodiment of wisdom and compassion is the greatest challenge spiritual seekers face. The truths we have come to understand need to find their visible expression in our lives. Our every thought, word, or action holds the possibility of being a living expression of clarity and love. It is not enough to be a possessor of wisdom. To believe ourselves to be custodians of truth is to become its opposite, is a direct path to becoming stale, self-righteous, or rigid. Ideas and memories do not hold liberating or healing power.

There is no such state as enlightened retirement, where we can live on the bounty of past attainments. Wisdom is alive only as long as it is lived, understanding is liberating only as long as it is applied. A bulging portfolio of spiritual experiences matters little if it does not have the power to sustain us through the inevitable moments of grief, loss, and change. Knowledge and achievements matter little if we do not yet know how to touch the heart of another and be touched.

—Christina Feldman and Jack Kornfield,
Stories of the Spirit, Stories of the Heart

The Buddha's teachings are unusual in that they explain at great length the nature of his enlightenment and the types of meditative disciplines he used to gain his insights. He left us a road map to enlightenment. Indeed, his chief motivation for teaching was to lead others to the spiritual awakening he experienced. Statements attributed to the Buddha make it very clear that all sentient beings have the capacity to become Buddhas, and that his own realizations occurred by practicing the Dharma he taught. Over the past 2,500 years the Buddha's teachings have been tested experientially by thousands of the greatest sages of Asia. Many have verified for themselves the Buddha's words and have achieved the same realizations he did.

—B. Alan Wallace, *Tibetan Buddhism from the Ground Up*

The Buddha's maps for the journey to wisdom and happiness are attractive to many people because they are so simple. Essentially, he taught that it doesn't make sense to upset ourselves about what is beyond our control. We don't get a choice about what hand we are dealt in this life. The only choice we have is our attitude about the cards we hold and the finesse with which we play our hand.

When the Buddha taught his ideas twenty-five hundred years ago, many people understood him so well as soon as they heard him that they were happy ever after. The people who didn't understand him immediately needed to practice meditation, and then they understood.

—Sylvia Boorstein, *It's Easier Than You Think*

For some, [the] task of coming back a thousand or ten thousand times in meditation may seem boring or even of questionable importance. But how many times have we gone away from the reality of our life?—perhaps a million or ten million times! If we wish to awaken, we have to find our way back here with our full being, our full attention. . . . In this way, meditation is very much like training a puppy. You put the puppy down and say, "Stay." Does the puppy listen? It gets up and it runs away. You sit the puppy back down again. "Stay." And the puppy runs away over and over again. Sometimes the puppy jumps up, runs over, and pees in the corner or makes some other mess. Our minds are much the same as the puppy, only they create even bigger messes. In training the mind, or the puppy, we have to start over and over again.

—Jack Kornfield, *A Path with Heart*

There are three integral factors in Buddhist meditation—morality, concentration, and wisdom. Those three factors grow together as your practice deepens. Each one influences the other, so you cultivate the three of them together, not one at a time. When you have the wisdom to truly understand a situation, compassion towards all the parties involved is automatic, and compassion means that you automatically restrain yourself from any thought, word, or deed that might harm yourself or others. Thus your behavior is automatically moral. It is only when you don't understand things deeply that you create problems. If you fail to see the consequences of your own action, you will blunder. The fellow who waits to become totally moral before he begins to meditate is waiting for a "but" that will never come. The ancient sages say that he is like a man waiting for the ocean to become calm so that he can go take a bath.

—Henepola Gunaratana, *Mindfulness in Plain English*

Concentration and mindfulness are distinctly different functions. They each have their role to play in meditation, and the relationship between them is definite and delicate. Concentration is often called one-pointedness of mind. It consists of forcing the mind to remain on one static point. Please note the word *force*. Concentration is pretty much a forced type of activity. It can be developed by force, by sheer unremitting willpower. And once developed, it retains some of that forced flavor. Mindfulness, on the other hand, is a delicate function leading to refined sensibilities. These two are partners in the job of meditation. Mindfulness is the sensitive one. . . . Mindfulness picks the objects of attention, and notices when the attention has gone astray. Concentration does the actual work of holding the attention steady on that chosen object. If either of these partners is weak, your meditation goes astray.

—Henepola Gunaratana, *Mindfulness in Plain English*

The basic objection to alcoholic drinks and [hallucinogenic] drugs lies in the fact that they distort the mental vision, if only temporarily; in such case it is not possible to preserve the vigilance and alertness which Buddhists should continuously practice. Possibly the best illustration of this distortion, even though very slight, may be taken from the experience of drivers of motor vehicles who are, as a rule, averse to taking any alcoholic drinks when driving or about to drive. . . . In view of certain current misapprehensions, it should be firmly stated that the use of hallucinogenic drugs for the purpose of attaining allegedly "higher" meditative states is highly dangerous and is a contravention of the Fifth Precept.

—Hammalawa Saddhatissa, *Buddhist Ethics*

The art of dharma practice requires commitment, technical accomplishment, and imagination. As with all arts, we will fail to realize its full potential if any of these three is lacking. The raw material of dharma practice is ourself and our world, which are to be understood and transformed according to the vision and values of the dharma itself. This is not a process of self- or world-transcendence, but one of self- and world-*creation*.

The denial of "self" challenges only the notion of a static self independent of body and mind—not the ordinary sense of ourself as a person distinct from everyone else. The notion of a static self is the primary obstruction to the realization of our unique potential as an individual being. By dissolving this fiction through a centered vision of the transiency, ambiguity, and contingency of experience, we are freed to create ourself anew.

—Stephen Batchelor, *Buddhism Without Beliefs*

Ego is like a room of your own, a room with a view with the temperature and the smells and the music that you like. You want it your own way. You'd just like to have a little peace; you'd like to have a little happiness, you know, just "gimme a break."

But the more you think that way, the more you try to get life to come out so that it will always suit you, the more your fear of other people and what's outside your room grows. Rather than becoming more relaxed, you start pulling down the shades and locking the door. When you do go out, you find the experience more and more unsettling and disagreeable. You become touchier, more fearful, more irritable than ever. The more you just try to get it your way, the less you feel at home.

—Pema Chödrön, *Start Where You Are*

Shantideva characterizes the hold our delusions have over us as follows:

> Although my enemies of hatred, attachment and so forth have neither weapons, legs nor arms, still they harm and torture me and treat me like a slave.

According to the dharma our worst enemy is delusion. This refers to any mental factor that disturbs and harms our peaceful mind. If we wish to be free of all suffering we must be able to identify the various delusions and understand how they harm us. Generally we all try to be aware of our external enemies but we pay scant heed to the inner enemies infecting our own mind. If we do not recognize the delusions and see how they harm us, how can we ever overcome our suffering? Buddha identified the six root delusions that poison our mind as follows: (1) attachment, (2) anger, (3) pride, (4) ignorance, (5) deluded doubt and (6) wrong views.

—Geshe Kelsang Gyatso, *Meaningful to Behold*

"Physical form . . . is not the self. If physical form were the self, this body would not lend itself to dis-ease. One could get physical form to be like this and not be like that. But precisely because physical form is not the self, it lends itself to dis-ease. And one cannot get physical form to be like this and not be like that.

"Feeling is not the self. . . . Perception is not the self. . . . Mental processes are not the self. . . .

"Consciousness is not the self. If consciousness were the self, this consciousness would not lend itself to dis-ease. One could get consciousness to be like this and not be like that. But precisely because consciousness is not the self, it lends itself to dis-ease. And one cannot get consciousness to be like this and not be like that."

—Bhikkhu Thanissaro, *The Mind Like Fire Unbound*

Dukkha is our best teacher. It will not be persuaded by any pleading of misery to let go of us. If we say to a human teacher, "I don't feel well . . . ," the teacher may reply, "I am very sorry, but if you want to go home, then you must go." If we say to *dukkha,* "Look, I don't feel well . . . I want to go home," *dukkha* says, "That's fine, but I am coming along." There is no way to say goodbye to it unless and until we have transcended our reactions. This means that we have looked *dukkha* squarely in the eye and see it for what it is: a universal characteristic of existence and nothing else. The reason we are fooled is that because this life contains so many pleasant occasions and sense contacts, we think if we could just keep this pleasantness going *dukkha* would never come again. We try over and over again to make this happen, until in the end we finally see that the pleasantness cannot continue because the law of impermanence intervenes. . . . So we continue our search for something new, because everybody else is doing it too.

—Ayya Khema, *When the Iron Eagle Flies*

A primary cause of suffering is delusion: our inability, because of a subtly willful blindness, to see things the way they truly are but instead in a distorted way. The world is in fact a seamless and dynamic unity: a single living organism that is constantly undergoing change. Our minds, however, chop it up into separate, static bits and pieces, which we then try mentally and physically to manipulate.

One of the mind's most dear creations is the idea of the person and, closest to home, of a very special person which each one of us calls "I": a separate, enduring ego or self. In a moment, then, the seamless universe is cut in two. There is "I"—and there is all the rest. That means conflict—and pain, for "I" cannot control that fathomless vastness against which it is set. It will try, of course, as a flea might pit itself against an elephant, but it is a vain enterprise.

—John Snelling, *Elements of Buddhism*

The expression of emptiness is love, because emptiness means "emptiness of self." When there is no self, there is no other. That duality is created by the idea of self, of I, of ego. When there's no self, there is a unity, a communion. And without the thought of "I'm loving someone," love becomes the natural expression of that oneness.

—Joseph Goldstein, *The Experience of Insight*

[T]he degree of love we manifest determines the degree of spaciousness and freedom we can bring to life's events.

Imagine taking a very small glass of water and putting into it a teaspoon of salt. Because of the small size of the container, the teaspoon of salt is going to have a big impact upon the water. However, if you approach a much larger body of water, such as a lake, and put into it that same teaspoonful of salt, it will not have the same intensity of impact, because of the vastness and openness of the vessel receiving it. Even when the salt remains the same, the spaciousness of the vessel receiving it changes everything.

We spend a lot of our lives looking for a feeling of safety or protection—we try to alter the amount of salt that comes our way. Ironically, the salt is the very thing that we cannot do anything about, as life changes and offers us repeated ups and downs. Our true work is to create a container so immense that any amount of salt, even a truckload, can come into it without affecting our capacity to receive it.

—Sharon Salzberg, *Lovingkindness*

Go to a party. Listen to the laughter, that brittle-tongued voice that says fun on the surface and fear underneath. Feel the tension, feel the pressure. Nobody really relaxes. They are faking it. Go to a ball game. Watch the fans in the stand. Watch the irrational fit of anger. Watch the uncontrolled frustration bubbling forth from people that masquerades under the guise of enthusiasm, or team spirit. Booing, catcalls and unbridled egotism in the name of team loyalty. Drunkenness, fights in the stands. These are people trying desperately to release tension from within. These are not people who are at peace with themselves. Watch the news on TV. Listen to the lyrics in popular songs. You find the same theme repeated over and over in variations. Jealousy, suffering, discontent, and stress.

Life seems to be a perpetual struggle, some enormous effort against staggering odds. And what is our solution to all this dissatisfaction? We get stuck in the "if only" syndrome.

—Henepola Gunaratana, *Mindfulness in Plain English*

Suzuki Roshi said, "Renunciation is not giving up the things of this world, but accepting that they go away." Everything is impermanent; sooner or later everything goes away. Renunciation is a state of nonattachment, acceptance of this going away. Impermanence is, in fact, just another name for perfection. Leaves fall; debris and garbage accumulate; out of the debris come flowers, greenery, things that we think are lovely. Destruction is necessary. A good forest fire is necessary. The way we interfere with forest fires may not be a good thing. Without destruction, there could be no new life; and the wonder of life, the constant change, could not be. We must live and die. And this process is perfection itself.

All this change is not, however, what we had in mind. Our drive is not to appreciate the perfection of the universe. Our personal drive is to find a way to endure in our unchanging glory forever. . . . Who hasn't noticed the first gray hair and thought, "Uh-oh."

—Charlotte Joko Beck, *Everyday Zen*

Renunciation does not have to be regarded as negative. I was taught that it has to do with letting go of holding back. What one is renouncing is closing down and shutting off from life. You could say that renunciation is the same thing as opening to the teachings of the present moment. . . .

Renunciation is realizing that our nostalgia for wanting to stay in a protected, limited, petty world is insane. Once you begin to get the feeling of how big the world is and how vast our potential for experiencing life is, then you really begin to understand renunciation. When we sit in meditation, we feel our breath as it goes out, and we have some sense of willingness just to be open to the present moment. Then our minds wander off into all kinds of stories and fabrications and manufactured realities, and we say to ourselves, "It's thinking." We say that with a lot of gentleness and a lot of precision. Every time we are willing to let the story line go, and every time we are willing to let go at the end of the outbreath, that's fundamental renunciation: learning how to let go of holding on and holding back.

—Pema Chödrön, *Tricycle: The Buddhist Review,* Vol. I, #1

Some students of religion postpone their lives and then wake up one day and say, "Wait a minute, here I am forty years old and I don't have a spouse or a career. What am I going to do when I grow up?" They have let things back up as they wait to be enlightened, or to be settled in mind. This shows a misunderstanding of the nature of practice.

Right practice, the ninth step of the Eightfold Path, does not involve waiting for the psyche to ripen. The clock is ticking. Right Practice is taking yourself in hand. For the lay student, it can include college, a career, and a family. It is to get on with living.

—Robert Aitken, *Encouraging Words*

To say that Buddhism is transitory, insubstantial and conditional is merely to restate its own understanding of the nature of things. Yet its teachings endlessly warn of the deeply engrained tendency to overlook this reality. . . . Instead of seeing a particular manifestation of the Dharma as a living spiritual tradition of possibilities contingent upon historical and cultural circumstances, one reifies it into an independently existent, self-sufficient fact, resistant to change.

Living continuity requires both change and constancy. Just as in the course of a human life, a person changes from a child to an adolescent to an adult while retaining a recognizable identity (both internally through memory and externally through recurring physical and behavioral traits), so does a spiritual tradition change through the course of its history while retaining a recognizable identity through a continuous affirmation of its axiomatic values. Thus Buddhism will retain its identity as a tradition as long as its practitioners continue to center their lives around the Buddha, Dharma and Sangha and affirm its basic tenets. But precisely how such commitment and affirmation are expressed in different times and places can differ wildly.

The survival of Buddhism today is dependent on its continuing ability to adapt.

—Stephen Batchelor, *The Awakening of the West*

In conclusion, let me share with you a short prayer which gives me great inspiration and determination:

> For as long as space endures,
> And for as long as living beings remain,
> Until then may I, too, abide
> To dispel the misery of the world.

—The Dalai Lama, "Nobel Peace Prize Lecture," in
The Dalai Lama: A Policy of Kindness,
edited by Sidney Piburn

Acknowledgments

We gratefully acknowledge the following publishers and authors who have granted us permission to publish excerpts from their works. Every reasonable effort has been made to obtain appropriate permission to reprint material.

Aitken, Robert. From *Encouraging Words* by Robert Aitken. Copyright © 1993 by Robert Aitken. Reprinted by permission of Pantheon Books, a division of Random House, Inc.

Aoyama, Shundo. *Zen Seeds*. Published by Kosei Publishing Co., Tokyo, in 1990. Reprinted by permission of Kosei Publishing Co., Tokyo.

Batchelor, Stephen. Reprinted from *The Awakening of the West: The Encounter of Buddhism and Western Culture* (1994) by Stephen Batchelor with permission of Parallax Press, Berkeley, California.

Batchelor, Stephen. *Buddhism Without Beliefs: A Contemporary Guide to Awakening*. Copyright © 1997 by Stephen Batchelor and The Buddhist Ray, Inc. Published by Riverhead Books, a member of Penguin Putnam Inc.

Beck, Charlotte Joko and Steven A. Smith. *Nothing Special: Living Zen*. Copyright © 1993 by Charlotte Joko Beck. Reprinted by permission of HarperCollins Publishers, Inc.

Beck, Charlotte Joko and Steve Smith. *Everyday Zen*. Copyright © 1989 by Charlotte Joko Beck and Steve Smith. Reprinted by permission of HarperCollins Publishers, Inc.

Bercholz, Samuel, *Entering the Stream*. Copyright © 1993 by Shambhala Publications. Published by Shambhala Publications, Inc., 300 Massachusetts Avenue, Boston, MA 02115.

Bodhi, Bhikkhu. Copyright © 1995 by Bhikkhu Bodhi. Reprinted from *The Middle Length Discourses of the Buddha: A New Translation of the Majjhima Nikaya* with permission of Wisdom Publications, 361 Newberry Street, Boston, Massachusetts, USA.

Boorstein, Sylvia. *It's Easier Than You Think: The Buddhist Way to Happiness* by Sylvia Boorstein. Copyright © 1995 by Sylvia Boorstein. Reprinted by permission of HarperCollins Publishers, Inc.

Hanh, Thich Nhat. Reprinted from *The Heart of Understanding: Commentaries on the Prajñaparamita Heart Sutra* (1988) by Thich Nhat Hanh with permission of Parallax Press, Berkeley, California.

Hanh, Thich Nhat. *Interbeing: Fourteen Guidelines for Engaged Buddhism.* Copyright © 1987. Reprinted by permission of Parallax Press, Berkeley, California.

Hanh, Thich Nhat. Reprinted from *Present Moment, Wonderful Moment: Mindfulness Verses for Daily Living* (1990) by Thich Nhat Hanh with permission of Parallax Press, Berkeley, California.

Hanh, Thich Nhat. Reprinted from *Our Appointment with Life: Buddha's Teaching on Living in the Present* (1990) by Thich Nhat Hanh with permission of Parallax Press, Berkeley, California.

Hanh, Thich Nhat. From *Peace Is Every Step: The Path of Mindfulness in Everyday Life* by Thich Nhat Hanh. Copyright © 1991 by Thich Nhat Hanh. Used by permission of Bantam Books, a division of Bantam Doubleday Dell Publishing Group, Inc.

Hanh, Thich Nhat. *Zen Keys: A Guide to Zen Practice* by Thich Nhat Hanh. Copyright © 1974 by Doubleday, a division of Bantam Doubleday Dell Publishing Group, Inc. Used by permission of Doubleday, a division of Bantam Doubleday Dell Publishing Group, Inc.

Herrigel, Eugen. *Zen and the Art of Archery.* Copyright © 1971. Reprinted by permission of Vintage/Random House, Inc.

Kabat-Zinn, Jon. Reprinted from *Wherever You Go, There You Are: Mindfulness Meditation in Everyday Life* by Jon Kabat-Zinn. Copyright © 1994 by Jon Kabat-Zinn. Reprinted with permission by Hyperion.

Khema, Ayya. From *When the Iron Eagle Flies: Buddhism for the West* by Ayya Khema. Copyright ©1991 by Ayya Khema. Published by Arkana. Reproduced by permisison of Penguin Books Ltd.

Kokushi, Muso. From *Dream Conversations* by Muso Kokushi, translated by Thomas Cleary, copyright © 1994. Reprinted by arrangement with Shambhala Publications, Inc., 300 Massachusetts Avenue, Boston, MA 02115.

Kornfield, Jack. From *Living Dharma* by Jack Kornfield, copyright © 1977, 1996. Reprinted by arrangement with Shambhala Publications, Inc., 300 Massachusetts Avenue, Boston, MA 02115.

Kornfield, Jack. From *A Path with Heart* by Jack Kornfield. Copyright © 1993 by Jack Kornfield. Used by permission of Bantam Books, a division of Bantam Doubleday Dell Publishing Group, Inc.

Kraft, Kenneth. *Inner Peace, World Peace.* Copyright © 1992. State University of New York Press, State University Plaza, Albany, NY 12246.

Subject Guide

Buddha, statements of: 1/4, 2/7, 2/12, 2/14, 2/16, 2/18, 2/20, 2/21, 2/22, 2/23, 2/26, 2/27, 3/1, 3/15, 3/16, 5/7, 5/8, 9/2, 9/6, 9/20, 10/9, 10/10, 10/11, 10/12, 10/13, 11/22, 12/8, 12/20

Buddhist practice: 1/1, 1/2, 1/3, 1/12, 1/17, 1/25, 1/30, 1/31, 2/4, 2/6, 2/11, 3/8, 3/9, 3/10, 3/13, 3/14, 4/18, 4/19, 5/4, 5/5, 5/7, 5/8, 5/9, 5/10, 5/11, 5/16, 6/1, 6/11, 6/14, 6/15, 6/18, 7/7, 7/21, 7/25, 7/26, 7/30, 8/12, 8/19, 8/24, 8/25, 9/11, 9/15, 9/17, 11/2, 11/6, 12/4, 12/6, 12/7, 12/11, 12/12, 12/13, 12/15, 12/30, 12/31

Eightfold Path: 2/18, 2/19, 2/28, 6/1, 12/29

Emptiness: 1/29, 5/21, 7/16, 9/4, 9/5, 9/6

Engaged Buddhism: 1/5, 5/14, 5/15, 5/19, 7/6, 7/29, 8/2, 9/27, 10/6, 11/20

Enlightenment: 1/4, 1/5, 1/6, 1/7, 1/8, 2/9, 2/10, 3/1, 4/3, 4/4, 5/17, 6/6, 6/9, 6/10, 7/17, 7/18, 7/19, 7/31, 8/16, 8/30, 9/12, 9/13, 9/14, 9/15, 9/16, 9/17, 10/5, 12/8, 12/9, 12/10, 12/12

Four Noble Truths: 1/9, 1/10, 1/11, 2/15, 2/16, 2/18, 3/15, 3/16, 3/17, 3/21, 4/5, 4/24, 5/18, 5/19, 6/7, 6/8, 6/16, 7/1, 8/4, 9/28, 10/13, 10/25, 10/27, 10/28, 11/15, 12/22, 12/23, 12/26

Hindrances: 6/22, 6/23

Karma: 1/21, 1/28, 3/24, 3/25, 3/30, 3/31, 4/29, 4/30, 5/1, 6/4, 7/13, 7/22, 7/23, 8/1, 8/2, 9/20, 9/23, 11/21, 11/22, 11/28, 11/29, 11/30

Metta: 2/14, 2/29, 3/25, 4/7, 4/12, 6/5, 6/13, 7/11, 7/20, 7/27, 9/29, 10/26, 11/8, 11/9, 11/10, 12/25

Precepts: 1/25, 1/26, 3/22, 4/13, 4/14, 4/16, 8/3, 9/30, 10/1, 10/19, 12/17

Refuges: 5/26, 6/1, 6/2, 6/3, 6/4, 6/7, 9/24, 12/8

Right Action: 1/25, 1/26, 2/23, 3/22, 3/28, 3/29, 3/31, 4/13, 4/14, 4/18, 5/13, 5/14, 9/21, 9/22, 9/30, 10/1, 10/2, 10/21, 1023, 11/20

Right Concentration/Meditation practice: 1/13, 1/14, 1/15, 1/16, 1/18, 1/19, 1/20, 2/27, 3/4, 3/5, 3/6, 3/10, 3/11, 3/24, 4/2, 4/8, 4/9, 4/10, 4/11, 5/2, 5/29, 5/30, 6/22, 8/8, 8/10, 10/29, 10/30, 10/31, 11/11, 11/16, 11/23, 12/14, 12/15

Right Effort: 2/1, 2/3, 2/4, 2/5, 2/8, 2/14, 2/25, 2/29, 4/1, 4/2, 4/20, 4/22, 4/23, 5/12, 5/25, 6/12, 6/22, 6/23, 8/9, 9/18, 11/13

Right Livelihood: 2/13, 2/23, 5/22, 5/23, 5/24, 5/25, 8/21, 8/22, 8/23, 12/1, 12/2, 12/3

Right Mindfulness: 1/17, 1/18, 2/27, 3/1, 3/2, 3/3, 3/4, 3/5, 3/6, 3/7, 3/11, 3/12, 3/19, 3/20, 3/27, 4/9, 4/10, 4/11, 4/25, 4/26, 4/27, 5/1, 5/6, 5/9, 5/28, 6/17, 6/21, 6/24, 6/25, 6/26, 6/27, 6/28, 6/29, 7/12, 8/26, 8/27, 8/31, 9/9, 9/10, 9/18, 9/19, 10/8, 10/30, 11/1, 11/25, 11/26, 12/5, 12/16, 12/21

Right Speech: 2/22, 4/6, 4/15, 4/16, 4/17, 10/16, 10/17, 10/18

Right Thought: 1/24, 2/2, 2/5, 2/10, 2/12, 2/21, 2/26, 3/23, 3/24, 3/26, 4/21, 4/28, 5/27, 6/19, 6/20, 6/23, 7/5, 7/9, 7/10, 7/14, 7/15, 7/16, 8/19, 10/7, 10/9, 10/10, 10/11, 10/12, 10/13, 10/14, 10/15, 11/12

Right Understanding: 1/4, 1/5, 1/6, 1/7, 1/8, 1/27, 1/28, 2/17, 2/20, 3/23, 3/24, 3/25, 3/30, 3/31, 4/1, 4/6, 4/26, 4/27, 4/29, 4/30, 5/1, 5/2, 5/3, 5/31, 6/5, 7/1, 7/2, 7/3, 7/4, 7/24, 7/28, 8/3, 8/4, 8/5, 8/6, 8/7, 8/14, 8/15, 8/18, 8/28, 8/29, 9/1, 9/2, 9/3, 9/5, 9/8, 10/2, 10/3, 10/20, 10/21, 10/22, 10/25, 11/7, 11/15, 11/16, 11/17, 11/18, 11/19, 11/24, 11/27, 12/27, 12/28

Self–Not Self: 1/21, 1/22, 1/23, 3/18, 5/20, 5/29, 6/14, 6/30, 7/1, 7/8, 7/16, 8/11, 8/13, 8/17, 9/25, 9/26, 9/27, 10/22, 10/24, 10/25, 11/3, 11/4, 11/5, 12/18, 12/19, 12/20, 12/24